THE PORT CHICAGO 50

STEVE SHEINKIN

THE PORT CHICAGO 50

DISASTER, MUTINY,
AND
THE FIGHT FOR CIVIL RIGHTS

SQUARE
FISH

Roaring Brook Press/New York

For Robert Allen, who has done so much
to keep this story alive

SQUARE
FISH

An imprint of Macmillan Publishing Group, LLC
175 Fifth Avenue
New York, NY 10010
mackids.com

THE PORT CHICAGO 50. Copyright © 2014 by Steve Sheinkin.
All rights reserved. Printed in the United States of America by
LSC Communications, Harrisonburg, Virginia.

Square Fish and the Square Fish logo are trademarks of Macmillan and
are used by Roaring Brook Press under license from Macmillan.

Our books may be purchased in bulk for promotional, educational, or business
use. Please contact your local bookseller or the Macmillan Corporate and
Premium Sales Department at (800) 221-7945 ext. 5442 or
by e-mail at MacmillanSpecialMarkets@macmillan.com.

Library of Congress Cataloging-in-Publication Data

Sheinkin, Steve.
  The Port Chicago 50 : disaster, mutiny, and the fight for civil rights / Steve Sheinkin.
    pages cm
  Includes bibliographical references and index.
    ISBN 978-1-250-07349-5 (paperback)   ISBN 978-1-59643-983-2 (ebook)
  1. World War, 1939–1945—Participation, African American—Juvenile literature.
  2. Port Chicago Mutiny, Port Chicago, Calif., 1944—Juvenile literature.
  3. Port Chicago Mutiny Trial, San Francisco, Calif., 1944—Juvenile literature.
  4. United States. Navy—African Americans—History—20th century—Juvenile
  literature.   5. African American sailors—History—20th century—Juvenile
  literature.   6. African Americans—Civil rights—History—20th century—Juvenile
  literature.   I. Title.
  D810.N4S44 2013
  940.54'5308996073079463—dc23
                                                              2013013452

Originally published in the United States by Roaring Brook Press
First Square Fish Edition: 2017
Square Fish logo designed by Filomena Tuosto

5   7   9   10   8   6

AR: 6.7 / LEXILE: 950L

The Port Chicago 50

Julius J. Allen

Mack Anderson

Douglas G. Anthony

William E. Banks

Arnett Baugh

Morris Berry

Martin A. Bordenave

Ernest D. Brown

Robert L. Burage

Mentor G. Burns

Zack E. Credle

Jack P. Crittenden

Hayden R. Curd

Charles L. David, Jr.

Bennon Dees

George W. Diamond

Kenneth C. Dixon

Julius Dixson

John H. Dunn

Melvin W. Ellis

William Fleece

James Floyd

Ernest J. Gaines

John L. Gipson

Charles C. Gray

Ollie E. Green

Harry E. Grimes

Herbert Havis

Charles N. Hazzard

Frank L. Henry

Richard W. Hill

Theodore King

Perry L. Knox

William H. Lock

Edward L. Longmire

Miller Matthews

Augustus P. Mayo

Howard McGee

Lloyd McKinney

Alphonso McPherson

Freddie Meeks

Cecil Miller

Fleetwood H. Postell

Edward Saunders

Cyril O. Sheppard

Joseph R. Small

Willie C. Suber

Edward L. Waldrop

Charles S. Widemon

Albert Williams, Jr.

"At some time, every Negro in the armed services asks himself what he is getting for the supreme sacrifice he is called upon to make."   —*Pittsburgh Courier*, November 9, 1944

CONTENTS

FIRST HERO • 1

THE POLICY • 5

PORT CHICAGO • 16

WORK AND LIBERTY • 26

THE LAWYER • 39

HOT CARGO • 47

THE EXPLOSION • 58

THE INQUIRY • 64

COLUMN LEFT • 78

PRISON BARGE • 87

THE FIFTY • 93

TREASURE ISLAND • 104

PROSECUTION • 114

JOE SMALL • 123

THE VERDICT • 133

HARD LABOR • 143

SMALL GOES TO SEA • 153

EPILOGUE: CIVIL RIGHTS HEROES • 159

SOURCE NOTES • 171

LIST OF WORKS CITED • 186

ACKNOWLEDGMENTS • 192

PICTURE CREDITS • 194

INDEX • 195

FIRST HERO

HE WAS GATHERING dirty laundry when the bombs started falling.

It was early on the morning of December 7, 1941, at the U.S. naval base at Pearl Harbor, Hawaii, and Mess Attendant Dorie Miller had just gone on duty aboard the battleship USS *West Virginia*. A six-foot-three, 225-pound Texan, Miller was the ship's heavyweight boxing champ. But his everyday duties were somewhat less challenging. As one of the ship's African American mess attendants, he cooked and cleaned for the white sailors.

Miller was below deck, picking up clothes, when the first torpedo slammed into the side of the *West Virginia*. Sirens shrieked and a voice roared over the loudspeaker:

"Japanese are attacking! All hands, General Quarters!"

Miller ran to his assigned battle station, an ammunition magazine—and saw it had already been blown apart.

He raced up to the deck and looked up at a bright blue sky streaked with enemy planes and falling bombs. Japan's massive attack had taken the base by surprise, and thunderous explosions were rocking American ships all over the harbor. Two direct hits cracked through the deck of the *West Virginia*, sending flames and shrapnel flying.

Amid the smoke and chaos, an officer saw Miller and shouted for him to help move the wounded. Miller began lifting men, carrying them farther from the spreading fires.

Then he spotted a dead gunner beside an anti-aircraft machine gun. He'd never been instructed in the operation of this weapon. But he'd seen it used. That was enough.

Jumping behind the gun, Miller tilted the barrel up and took aim at a Japanese plane. "It wasn't hard," he'd later say. "I just pulled the trigger, and she worked fine."

As Miller blasted away, downing at least one enemy airplane, several more torpedoes blew gaping holes in the side of the *West Virginia*. The ship listed sharply to the left as it took on water.

The captain, who lay dying of a belly wound, ordered, "Abandon ship!"

Sailors started climbing over the edge of the ship, leaping into the water. Miller scrambled around the burning, tilting deck, helping wounded crewmembers escape the sinking ship before jumping to safety himself.

After the battle, an officer who had witnessed Miller's bravery recommended him for the Navy Cross, the highest decoration given by the Navy. "For distinguished devotion to duty," declared Miller's official Navy Cross citation, "extraordinary courage and disregard for his own personal safety during the attack on the Fleet in Pearl Harbor."

In early 1942, soon after the United States had entered World

Admiral Chester Nimitz pins the Navy Cross on Dorie Miller, May 27, 1942.

War II, Admiral Chester Nimitz personally pinned the medal to Miller's chest. "This marks the first time in this conflict that such high tribute has been made in the Pacific Fleet to a member of his race," Nimitz declared. "I'm sure that the future will see others similarly honored for brave acts."

And then Dorie Miller, one of the first American heroes of World War II, went back to collecting laundry. He was still just a mess attendant.

It was the only position open to black men in the United States Navy.

THE POLICY

THE DAY AFTER JAPAN ATTACKED Pearl Harbor, the United States declared war on Japan. Japan's powerful ally, Germany, responded by declaring war on the United States. World War II was already raging across Europe, Africa, and Asia. Now the United States had officially entered the biggest war in human history.

New York World-Telegram

7TH SPORTS
LATEST RACING
Results on Page 26.

PRICE THREE CENTS

Local Forecast: Light rains tonight, somewhat higher temperatures than last night; tomorrow cloudy followed by clearing, cooler than today.

NEW YORK, MONDAY, DECEMBER 8, 1941.

VOL. 74—NO. 135—IN TWO SECTIONS—SECTION ONE

1500 DEAD IN HAWAII
Congress Votes War on Japan;
Manila Bases Bombed Again

"We are now fighting to maintain our right to live among our world neighbors in freedom," President Franklin D. Roosevelt told Americans in a radio address from the White House. "We are now in the midst of a war, not for conquest, not for vengeance, but for a world in which this nation, and all that this nation represents, will be safe for our children."

Trucks with roof-mounted speakers cruised slowly through American cities, blaring the call to arms: "Patriotic, red-blooded Americans! Join the Navy and help Uncle Sam hit back!"

For black Americans this was not so simple. When they volunteered to fight as sailors, they were reminded of the Navy's longstanding policy. They could serve on ships only as mess attendants.

It was a policy as old as the country itself.

When George Washington took command of the Continental

Emanuel Leutze's 1851 painting, Washington Crossing the Delaware, accurately depicts a mixed-race regiment, with a black soldier rowing to Washington's right.

Army in 1775, he told recruiters to stop signing up black soldiers. The fact is, black volunteers had *already* fought in the war's opening battles at Lexington, Concord, and Bunker Hill. But slave owners objected that arming African Americans could lead to slave rebellions, and Washington agreed not to accept more black soldiers. Two years of losing battles to the British, and soldiers to desertion and disease, changed the commander's perspective. Washington needed men, no matter the color. Eventually, about 5,000 African Americans helped win the American Revolution.

The pattern was repeated soon after the Civil War erupted in 1861. At first the United States Army would not accept black men, fearing that to do so would offend the slave states that were still in the Union. Then, as the war dragged on, and the Union's need for fighting men grew increasingly desperate, the policy changed. More than 200,000 black soldiers fought to save the Union and end slavery— but they did so in segregated units, led by white officers.

In the Spanish-American War, future president Teddy Roosevelt became a national hero for leading the charge up Cuba's San Juan Hill. Actually, hundreds of African American soldiers were charging up the hill too, in separate, segregated units. By the time they reached the top, white and black soldiers were all mixed together, and together they took the hill. But when newspapers reported on the victory, Roosevelt and his white volunteers got the credit.

More than 350,000 African Americans served in World War I, nearly all in segregated labor battalions. They drove trucks, dug trenches, buried bodies. The military based its policy of using African Americans as laborers on the prejudiced

assumption—one already decisively disproven by history—that black men would not make good combat soldiers.

"Poor Negroes!" one American general wrote in his diary during the war. "Everyone feeling and saying that they are worthless as soldiers."

Tellingly, several African American regiments wound up under the command of the French army, where they were given a fair shot to fight, and fought well. One black regiment from New York, nicknamed the Harlem Hellfighters, spent 191 days in combat—longer than any white American unit. They won a pile of medals, and returned to New York City as heroes. But the policy of the American military did not change.

At the time of the attack on Pearl Harbor, just 5,000 African Americans served in the entire U.S. Navy, all as messmen. The Army offered slightly better opportunities in terms of training and access to promotion—but remained strictly segregated. The Marines and Army Air Corps (later renamed the Air Force) did not accept blacks at all until later in the war.

"This policy," declared the War Department, referring to segregation, "has proven satisfactory over a long period of years."

Satisfactory to the government, that is.

As the United States raced to prepare for global combat, civil rights groups challenged the Navy to abolish its racial restrictions. Secretary of the Navy Frank Knox insisted there was nothing he could do.

True, there was an obvious contradiction in a nation fighting for freedom while denying it to its own citizens in the military.

The Harlem Hellfighters celebrate their arrival home from World War I in 1919.

Secretary of the Navy Frank Knox at his desk in 1943.

But, Secretary Knox explained, segregation and racism were deeply rooted facts of life in American society. These problems were not created by the military and were not the military's problems to solve. Aboard ships, men were crammed into close quarters, making it impossible to keep the races segregated. Neither could they be integrated, Knox argued, because white sailors wouldn't work well with black sailors, and certainly wouldn't take commands from them. To desegregate the Navy, therefore, would hurt the war effort.

Knox concluded the only solution was to keep black men,

other than those working as servants, off ships. The secretary insisted he was not a racist—simply a realist.

President Roosevelt accepted Knox's logic, agreeing that this was no time to desegregate the Navy. "To go the whole way at one fell swoop," he told Knox, "would seriously impair the general average efficiency of the Navy."

But Roosevelt was also a politician, always looking ahead to the next election. He counted on strong support from African American voters, and was getting pressure from black leaders to do *something* about the military's racial policies. So the president did what politicians often do—he looked for a compromise.

Secretary Knox unveiled the policy change in April 1942. The Navy would now begin accepting black volunteers for training as sailors, he announced. It sounded good, until you read the details. Black men could serve as sailors, but they'd be limited to low ranks; and they still could not serve aboard ships at sea, except as mess attendants.

African Americans were not impressed.

"In its abrupt announcement of a change of policy, the Navy department actually insults the intelligence of the Negroes it should seek to enlist," charged an editorial in the *Louisville Defender*, an African American–owned newspaper.

"It is difficult not to feel disgusted at the tricky, evasive, hypocritical manner in which the Secretary of the Navy has dealt with this problem," added a scathing editorial in another black paper, the *Pittsburgh Courier.* Roosevelt spoke in soaring phrases about America's battle to preserve freedom and democracy around the globe—but where were those ideals here at home? "If Negro youth are not good enough to fight alongside their white fellow Americans on land and sea in defense of their country, then this talk of democracy is hollow and meaningless."

In spite of the protests, the Navy went ahead with its plan.

And, in spite of the restrictions, plenty of young African Americans were eager to serve. That was certainly true of many of the men who would find themselves at a remote California naval base called Port Chicago.

In a speech at his high school graduation, seventeen-year-old Jack Crittenden spoke of Dorie Miller's inspiring heroism at Pearl Harbor. "All our men are facing the same enemy under the same flag," he told fellow students. "And when more black men are given the opportunity to serve their country, they will prove themselves worthy of the trust placed in them. Give them a chance!"

A Chicago teenager named Percy Robinson felt the same way. "The feeling was that we wanted to go in," Robinson said of himself and his friends. "We wanted to serve, and we wanted to get into combat, because all we were ever taught is that we were cowards, not capable of competing with the white man."

"We felt patriotic toward our country," recalled Albert Williams, Jr., about his feelings when joining the Navy. "Cause this is our country too."

Martin Bordenave was so eager to get into the Navy that he lied about his age and enlisted at sixteen.

Robert Routh was seventeen—old enough to enlist with a parent's signature. Growing up on a Tennessee farm, in a home with no electricity or indoor plumbing, Routh set his mind on joining the military and building himself a brighter future.

"If you sign for me," he told his father, "I can help make the country a better place for us blacks."

Reluctantly, Routh's father drove his son to the recruiting station in Macon. A farm boy who'd never been near the ocean, Routh saw himself as a soldier, not a sailor. But by the time they got to the Army recruiting office, the place was closed.

Routh looked around. About thirty yards down the block, a uniformed man stood outside the Navy recruiting office.

"Will the Army open up any more today?" Routh called.

"Come down here!" the man shouted.

Routh walked toward the office. "Well, I was trying to volunteer for the Army," he said.

The recruiter told Routh and his father all about the new opportunities open in the U.S. Navy. Before he left the office, Routh was signed up.

Joseph Small's path to the Navy involved a bit of chance. Small was working as a truck driver in New Jersey when he got his draft notice. He and a friend went for their physicals. Both passed.

"What branch of the service do you want?" the doctor asked them.

Surprised to be given a choice, they both hesitated.

The doctor picked up a stamp marked ARMY and—*BAM*—brought it down on Small's friend's enlistment papers.

"All right soldier," he said. "Move out."

Then he picked up a stamp marked NAVY and—*BAM*—hit Small's papers.

That random stamp is an essential element of this story.

Before the war, Joe Small had been in the Civilian Conservation Corps, a government program providing jobs for young

July 1946

men during the Great Depression. It was in a New Jersey CCC camp, at the age of eighteen, that Small discovered a quality he hadn't known he possessed.

He was working with a crew, cutting brush in the woods, when two of the men started to argue. Small looked up and saw the guys stepping angrily toward each other, both raising their axes.

Without thinking, Small jumped between the men.

"You give me your ax," he demanded of one. Then he turned to the other. "And you give me your ax."

Small took the axes. The fight was over.

"Small, you have natural leadership ability," his boss told him. Small was made squad leader, with his own crew to supervise.

This became a pattern with Joe Small. He didn't go around asking for respect, but he just naturally commanded it. He didn't ask to be put in leadership roles, but people just naturally turned to him for advice, or to settle disputes, or to speak up to the bosses on their behalf. In the Navy, Small would display these same qualities, with the same results. The men in his division would look to him as a leader, a spokesman.

And it was to these same qualities that officers would point when they accused Joe Small of leading the largest mutiny in the history of the United States Navy.

Joe Small in uniform, 1946.

PORT CHICAGO

JOE SMALL AND THE OTHER RECRUITS were sent to the U.S. Naval Training Center at Great Lakes, Illinois, a sprawling complex on the banks of Lake Michigan. For many, just being away from home was an exciting experience.

"We were so young, not old enough to vote or to have a legal drink," remembered Robert Routh. "Many of us had done no more than embrace a girl."

"Most of us didn't know how to shave," Percy Robinson recalled. The food, at least, was decent. "We ate three squares a day, which we never did before, at least I never did."

That was the good news about life in the Navy. The bad news was that the men couldn't go anywhere at Great Lakes without being made to feel like unwelcome guests.

"The first thing they did," remembered a sailor named De-Witt Jameson, "was to start segregating us."

Percy Robinson described lining up for his first meal at Great Lakes. "There were two lines," he explained. He stood with the

Black recruits are inspected by an officer at Naval Training Station (NTS), Great Lakes, August 1943.

other black recruits. "So you look around, and there's another line over there that's all white." Robinson watched the white recruits march up to the main floor to eat. Then the black recruits were led downstairs to separate tables. Until that moment, he hadn't realized how completely segregated the Navy was going to be.

The black recruits were actually housed in their own separate camp, a brand new black-only training center, slapped together when the Navy announced its new policy of accepting black sailors. The Navy needed somewhere to train these men, but didn't want them mixing with white recruits at Great Lakes. Classes at Great Lakes were segregated, musical bands, sports teams—everything.

The attitude of the black camp's commander, Lieutenant Commander Daniel Armstrong, was typical of the times. He had his men decorate the base with murals of black naval heroes throughout history, from Dorie Miller all the way back to black sailors who served with Revolutionary captain John Paul Jones. The murals were Armstrong's way of honoring black sailors. But this same officer wouldn't allow black recruits at Great Lakes to compete with whites for spots in special schools that trained sailors to be electricians, radiomen, and mechanics. He didn't think they were smart enough, so he didn't even let them try.

Just how deeply ingrained was segregation? Absurdly, the military even segregated its blood supply. Military leaders knew there was no difference between the blood of black and white men. They knew it was a waste of time and money to store two separate blood supplies. But that was the tradition, and no one in power wanted to challenge it.

Sailors in formation on the parade ground at NTS, Great Lakes, 1943.

"Negro sailors—we were called Negroes—Negro sailors were not accepted as real seamen," remembered Robert Edwards, who came to Great Lakes from Brooklyn, New York, at the age of eighteen. Edwards never forgot the day Secretary of the Navy Knox came to visit Great Lakes.

"We stood on the parade grounds for about two hours, waiting for him to come by, and he went to all the white camps and inspected the white camps, and then left," Edwards remembered. "That didn't make us feel very proud or patriotic."

For twelve weeks, the black recruits exercised and marched and stood at attention. They scrubbed their barracks spotless and practiced on the rifle range and took swimming tests in the pool. They were never trained to handle explosives, but were not surprised by this.

They had no idea it was something they would soon need to know.

As boot camp neared an end, the men swapped guesses about where they'd be going next. Like most of them, Joe Small imagined himself joining the fight aboard a ship at sea. It's what he was being trained for—or so he believed.

Martin Bordenave felt the same. "When I first enlisted in the Navy, I loved the sea," he later said. "I expected to be a sailor, like any other sailor in the Navy."

Cyril Sheppard knew all about the Navy's history of using black men only as messmen. He wanted no part of it. "See, when I come to fight," he said, "I don't want to come fighting with pots and pans."

"Most of us, a lot of us, wanted to go overseas, and wanted to shoot, get into combat," agreed Percy Robinson. "We figured that by serving and fighting and dying in the service, that when we got back home, we would get better rights."

Think about that. Robinson felt he had to prove himself in combat in order to "win" rights already guaranteed to *all* citizens in the United States Constitution.

Spencer Sikes, a teenager from Florida, was so eager to join the fight he convinced his mother to sign him up for the Navy when he was just seventeen.

"We had expectations to go to sea on a big Navy ship," Sikes remembered. "The letdown was that once we reached our station, we found out that a lot of the things we had believed were a fantasy."

Now officially seamen in the United States Navy, the young men boarded trains headed west, with no idea where the Navy was sending them. In California, buses carried them through the gates of a naval base about thirty miles northeast of San Francisco. The buses climbed a series of tall hills covered with dry grass. From the top of the last hill, the men looked out at a flat stretch of land along the banks of the mile-wide Suisun Bay. There were a few wooden buildings scattered around the mostly empty space and a pier at the waterfront.

This was their new home, the Port Chicago Naval Magazine.

"Strange thing, to look at all this vast space," Robert Routh remembered of his first view of Port Chicago. "And very few trees. Coming from a farm area, this was really hard on me, to see so little foliage. Really, it was a sad place to look at."

"Big open place, and a dock," recalled Percy Robinson. "That's about all there was there."

"Dumpy looking place, way back there in the boondocks,"

said a sailor named Freddie Meeks, echoing the first impressions of many. "And you were kinda disappointed. Because I really wanted to go out on a ship."

The bigger disappointment was still to come.

After dropping off their gear in the barracks, the sailors jumped on trucks and were driven about a mile down to the waterfront. There they got their first look at the work they'd been brought to Port Chicago to do.

A huge Navy ship was docked alongside the long wooden pier, which stretched 1,200 feet into the bay. There were railroad tracks on the pier. Boxcars sat on the tracks. Crews of young sailors in dungarees and blue work shirts were hauling heavy bombs and crates of ammunition out of the train cars and loading them onto the ship.

All the officers standing on the pier and giving orders were white. All the sailors handling explosives were black.

Captain Nelson Goss, commanding officer at Port Chicago, was not pleased with the personnel the Navy was sending him. He didn't want black workers, or any minorities, if it could be avoided.

"Most of the men obtainable from these races do not compare favorably with those of the white race," he complained. His busy base had one mission: to load bombs and ammunition onto ships, and he felt that black workers could only do about 60 percent as much work as whites.

The feeling was mutual: Goss didn't want these men, and the men didn't want to be there. Sure, the work at Port Chicago was

Port Chicago sailors at work on the loading pier.

a vital part of the war effort. American forces battling Japan in the Pacific needed massive supplies of ammunition, and someone had to load it onto ships. But that didn't lessen the men's frustration at being denied a chance to serve at sea. Soon after arriving, Robert Routh heard fellow sailors grumbling in the barracks.

"Ship us anywhere," men muttered.

"We came to *fight*. Let us fight."

There was an even more immediate problem, though, and Joe Small spotted it right away. At Great Lakes the sailors had been taught nothing about the safe handling of torpedo warheads or massive incendiary bombs. And, Small quickly realized, they were not going to be taught at Port Chicago either.

"The first time I saw any ammunition was the first time we were called out of the barracks and lined up and marched to the dock," Small recalled. "Our specific jobs were explained, and we took it from there as best we could."

The white officers at Port Chicago had been given a brief course on the safe handling of bombs and ammunition. They'd also spent a few hours at ports on San Francisco Bay, watching professional stevedores at work loading ships. That was the extent of their training.

It was more than the black sailors got.

The Navy never even gave the men any kind of written manual describing how to handle bombs safely. No such manual existed. Some safety regulations were posted on sheets of paper at the pier, but not in the barracks, where the men might actually have had time to read them; the officers didn't think the black sailors would be able to understand written regulations.

"They just brought you in and showed you—taught you a little something and turned you loose," remembered Freddie Meeks.

"I didn't know what to do," Morris Soublet later said. "So

we improvised our own ways." Yes, there were white officers who were supposedly supervising the work. "But they didn't know any more of what to do than we did."

It was a recipe for disaster, and civilian stevedores in the Bay Area were horrified. They never let a worker handle explosives until he'd gained years of experience on the job. The longshoremen's union offered to send trained loaders to teach the Navy recruits. The Navy never responded.

From the moment they arrived at Port Chicago, most of the men lived in constant fear of a catastrophic explosion. Seventeen-year-old Spencer Sikes was convinced he'd die at the base.

"Boy, I'll never make it back home," he thought as he worked. "I'll never see my mom again."

WORK AND LIBERTY

CLINK . . . THUD . . . CLINK . . .

This was the annoying series of sounds that woke Joe Small almost every morning at Port Chicago. He'd open his eyes and check the clock—just 4:30.

He'd try to get a little more sleep, but the clinking and thudding would continue. Small didn't have to look out the window to know the cause. The guy they called T. J. was out there in the dark, pitching horseshoes in bare feet and boxers, his sneakers tied together and hung over his neck.

T. J. did this every morning, week after week. Small figured T. J. was angling for a Section Eight—a discharge given to men mentally unfit for service. Anything to get out of Port Chicago.

Whether Small got back to sleep or not, he was usually the next member of Division Four to get out of bed. He'd always been an early riser, and the other men quickly began counting on him to get them up and on their way to chow.

"All right, buddy," Small would say, moving from bunk to bunk, shaking heavy sleepers. "Let's go, buddy, get up."

He'd been like that from a young age.

"My father didn't believe in me depending on help," Small would later explain. "He taught us to be independent."

Growing up on his family's 80-acre farm in New Jersey, Joe handled jobs in the fields and around the house. "For instance I had the chore of bringing in the night pail every night," he said. With no indoor plumbing, the Smalls used an outhouse during the day—and at night, the pail. "And if I went to bed without getting that night pail in, if it was needed at any time of night, I went out and got it." Didn't matter what time it was, or what the weather was like. "I've gotten out of bed at 3:00 in the morning," he said, "in two foot of snow."

One afternoon, when Small was fourteen, he was hanging out at a roadside truck stop near his home, watching the big rigs come and go. A driver stepped out of the restaurant and saw the skinny teenager staring up at his truck, piled high with long logs. He thought he'd have some fun with the kid.

"You think you can move that?" the driver teased.

"Sure, I can," Small snapped back. "I can drive anything on wheels."

A slight exaggeration—he'd driven a tractor on his family's farm, but that's about it.

The driver smiled and pointed up to the cab. "The key's in it. Go ahead."

Small climbed in and took a quick look around. He started the engine, grabbed the shift stick, and wrestled the truck into first gear. Then, gently, he lowered his foot onto the gas pedal.

The driver looked up, stunned to see his rig begin rolling through the parking lot. He hollered for Small to stop.

Small's foot slammed on the brake. The jolt of the sudden stop sent one of the logs sliding forward; it smashed through the back window, sped past Small's head, crashed through the front windshield, and came to a stop sticking out from the front of the truck.

There was a short silence.

And then the driver erupted with a burst of curses, roaring so furiously he literally started hopping up and down. Small opened the cab door, jumped to the ground, and took off down the road.

Joe's father died a year later. The family scraped by, growing their own food, sometimes selling extra tomatoes and lettuce. But the Smalls needed income, and Joe stepped up.

In a local newspaper he saw that a furniture company was looking for truck drivers. He was just fifteen. He didn't have a driver's license, and didn't exactly know how to drive a truck. None of that stopped him. He walked into the furniture company's office and asked for the job.

"You got a license?"

"Yeah," Small said, tapping his hip pocket.

"All right, all right," said the manager, "as long as you got it."

Joe drove for the company for a year and finally got his driver's license when he turned sixteen. All the while, he tried to keep up with school. The schoolwork was no problem, but there was an irritating kid in his class, a white kid who thought it was funny to call black kids like Small "Smokey"—and then duck behind his 200-pound cousin.

Small was thin, about five foot seven, but never one to back down. He promised his tormentor he'd catch him one day when the big cousin wasn't around. He kept the promise. "I put a good whipping on him," Small recalled. "They gave me an alternative: either leave school or be sent to a reform school."

That was the end of Joe Small's formal education.

Small was twenty-two years old when he got to Port Chicago, a few years older than most of the men in his division. He had a bit more life experience than the other men, and the confidence that came with it.

"I demanded, I guess you could use that phrase, I *demanded* respect," Small later said, explaining how he came to be seen as the unofficial leader of his division. "I mean, I would tell a man, 'Shut up. You talk too much.' Look him straight in the eye, and that was it, and he'd get the opinion I meant what I said, and if he didn't shut up the consequences would be disastrous. And through that attitude I gained the respect of the men."

Small and the men had to be dressed and ready for work by 6:45 a.m., when their lieutenant's voice came blasting out of the speakers in the barracks: "Now hear this, now hear this! Division Four, Barracks B, fall out, fall out!"

From that moment, the men had exactly two minutes to line up in the street outside the barracks. As they were forming ranks, elbowing each other into place, Lieutenant Ernest Delucchi walked up to inspect his division. A schoolteacher in civilian life, Delucchi had joined the Navy when the war began. He was short, stocky, in his early thirties.

"He looked like an old guy," Percy Robinson remembered of Delucchi. "I didn't like him too well."

"He spent half the day wanting to knock somebody down," Cyril Sheppard recalled. "He was always challenging different guys: 'If you think you're big enough, come on out here, step forward' and all that kind of stuff."

"Very hot-tempered," Joe Small added. "If things didn't go his way, he was very quick to punish you for it."

Small managed to stay on Delucchi's good side, though. The lieutenant quickly recognized Small's leadership skills and assigned Small the job of marching outside the ranks and calling cadence.

"Left! Left! Left, right, left!" Small chanted as the division marched in rows, the pounding of boots on pavement falling into rhythm with his chant. After a short march, the men crowded into trucks—"cattle cars," the guys derisively joked—and rode down to the pier to begin another day's work.

Sailors march onto the Port Chicago pier to begin their work shift.

On the long pier leading out into the bay, the men divided into five groups of about twenty men each. The ships they loaded had five hatches, and each team loaded bombs into one of the hatches. Each team broke into two squads. One worked on the pier, one in the ship's hold—the huge, open storage area below deck.

Train tracks ran down from the base and out onto the pier, allowing boxcars full of explosives to roll onto the pier and stop beside the waiting ship.

Above and right: Sailors unload crates of ammunition from boxcars at the pier.

"We'd open the boxcar doors," Small described, "and the bombs would be stacked four, five, or six high inside the car."

A couple of men climbed in, crouching between the top layer of bombs and the roof of the car. Using long wooden planks, they set up a ramp from the top of the bombs down to the pier, about eight feet below. Others, meanwhile, hung mattresses on the side of the ship—to cushion the blow in case one of the 500-pound shells rolled too fast down the ramp, sped across the pier, and slammed into the side of the metal ship. It happened all the time.

"You'd hear this all day long: *BOOM! BOOM! BOOM-BOOM!*" Percy Robinson remembered.

"And that would almost give you a heart attack," said Freddie Meeks. Several times he asked the officers if there was any danger of an accidental explosion.

Their response was always the same: "Oh, no, don't worry about it."

Small heard this, but wasn't convinced. He asked his lieutenant for a more detailed answer. Delucchi took out a booklet, flipped to a diagram of the 500-pound bomb they were loading and pointed out the detonator, which was attached to the head of the bomb. It was the detonator that triggered the explosion by sending a spark into the TNT packed into the bomb. The bombs the men were loading didn't have the detonators attached yet.

"Won't concussion blow this thing up?" Small asked.

"Impossible," said Delucchi, pointing again to the diagram.

Once the bombs and crates of smaller ammunition made it down to the pier, the men rolled or lifted everything into nets. Each net was attached to a crane, which could be lifted by a motorized winch. Pulling levers in the winch, the winch operator lifted the sagging net into the air, guided it over the open hold of the ship, and lowered it down into the hold.

The crew in the hold unloaded the ammo in the ship. "You'd build yourself all the way up," one sailor explained, "just packing until you found yourself way up on top." After the first day of loading, the team would be working on top of a layer of bombs. They continued stacking explosives higher and higher until they reached the top of the hold.

At the very top, they loaded the "hot cargo," as the men called it—650-pound incendiary bombs. Unlike the other explosives stacked in the ship, these had their fuses already attached.

The men at Port Chicago described the scene on the loading pier as frantic, stressful, loud, chaotic—bombs rolling and clanking together, winch engines chugging and smoking, nets swinging through the air, sailors shouting and cursing, officers urging the men on.

"We were all afraid of an explosion," Small later said. "But there was very little that you could do about it. I mean, you had a day's work to do."

At first Joe Small worked on the pier, loading bombs with the rest of his crew. But he was fascinated by the winch operator job,

A winch is loaded before lifting heavy bombs over the high sides of a ship.

mainly because it was the only work on the dock that required any skill. While the others were finishing lunch, he'd slip off to sit in the machine, practicing with the levers. Drawing on years of experience as a truck driver, he soon learned how to handle the winch.

One day, one of the Division Four winch drivers had to leave for a medical emergency.

"Hey!" someone on the pier called out. "Where's the winch-man?"

Small stepped up. "I'll run it while he's gone."

He sat down, grabbed the levers, and got to work.

"So whenever they needed a replacement, they called on me," Small recalled. "And eventually, I took over the job completely."

That was typical Joe Small. Others in the division saw Small's skill and boldness, and responded to it.

"He should have been anything but what they had him doing," said a fellow sailor, expressing the common opinion in Division Four that Small should have been promoted to a position of more authority. "They just disregarded black people."

The men thought Small should at least be made a petty officer, the highest rank given to black sailors at Port Chicago. Lieutenant Delucchi told Small he had the ability for the job, but was still too young.

Small didn't get the promotion, or the private room and extra pay that went with it. But he got the responsibility, anyway. When Delucchi had a message to relay to the division, he went to Small instead of the division's petty officer. When the men had a question or complaint they wanted presented to Delucchi, they went to Small.

"Look, you got a petty officer," Small used to tell the men. "You got to talk to your petty officer."

The men would curse the petty officer, say he didn't know anything, didn't have the guts to speak up to the white officers. So Small would give in and help.

"And that just put me in deeper," he later said. He hadn't asked for the extra work, and didn't especially want it. "But I've never been one to shirk," he said. "Once I commit myself, I'll go through with it."

Each division worked an eight-hour shift, and then headed back to the barracks while another took over. Bright lights lit the pier at night, and the loading continued nonstop, twenty-four hours a day.

The men's lives were divided into eight-day segments. Three days of loading, then a "duty day"—laundry and other jobs around base—three more days of loading, then a day of liberty.

Like all the young sailors, Small treasured the chance to jump on a bus and get away from the base for a few hours, drink a beer in peace, maybe meet a girl. There was a town named Port Chicago about a mile from base, but it didn't have much to offer.

"It was just a one-street place," Robert Routh remembered; a few restaurants, a movie theater. "They didn't want blacks there at all. The townspeople didn't care for blacks."

The nearest place with any sort of nightlife was Pittsburg, but the city had only one street with bars at which black customers were welcome. When they got off the bus in Pittsburg, the Port Chicago sailors were expected to walk a specific five-block route through a white neighborhood, a maddening maze of turns, to reach the "permitted" Black Diamond Street.

"Other streets we were found on, we were accosted," Small

remembered. "We had to answer questions as to why we weren't where we were supposed to be."

The fact that these men were wearing the uniform of the United States Navy made no difference.

Most of the men preferred to head for the big cities of Oakland or San Francisco, though it meant a longer bus ride. One liberty day, riding a bus for Oakland, Robert Edwards struck up a friendly conversation with two white sailors headed the same way.

"Let's go over to the bar and have us a drink," one of the sailors said when the bus reached the station.

The men walked into a nearby joint and ordered three bottles of beer. The bartender set two bottles on the bar.

"What happened to my friend's beer?" asked one of the white sailors. "Aren't you going to give him a beer?"

The bartender said, "We don't serve niggers here."

Edwards turned and walked out alone. He got on a bus and headed back to Port Chicago.

"We're supposed to be fighting the same enemy," he thought. "I don't know who my enemy really is."

After that, he spent his liberty days on base, in his bunk with a novel.

When he'd joined the Navy, people told him, "You're fighting for your freedom!"

Now he wondered: "Where's the freedom?"

THE LAWYER

Robert edwards's experience was far from unique in World War II America.

Black newspapers received a steady stream of letters from African American soldiers and sailors describing the lousy treatment they were getting in the military.

"Here on the post we're treated like dogs," wrote one soldier from a segregated base in Colorado. He described lining up outside the chow hall with the other black soldiers, and being ordered to wait until the white men finished eating—and then being served cold leftovers.

Another soldier wrote from an Alabama base, where the movie theater had five seats reserved "for colored." If more than five black men wanted to see the film, they were out of luck. At a base in Georgia, black soldiers were woken up an hour before white soldiers—to clean the toilets in the white barracks.

At the Tuskegee Air Field in Alabama, the Army was training the country's first group of African American fighter pilots. It was an important step forward, yet even there, black pilots were confronted with "white" and "colored" signs over the toilets.

Segregation was even crueler in the towns near military bases, especially in the South. In a letter to *Yank*, a weekly newspaper written by American soldiers, Corporal Rupert Trimmingham described a scene that became famous as a symbol of the hypocrisy of segregation in an army that was fighting for freedom around the world.

Trimmingham was traveling to a new base with a group of black soldiers. Their train stopped in a small Louisiana town, and the next train didn't leave until morning. The men walked into town and tried to buy a meal. Not a single restaurant would serve them.

Finally, the lunchroom in the train station agreed to feed them—but only if they'd come around to the back entrance and eat, standing up, in the kitchen.

To Trimmingham this was galling enough. Then came the bigger slap.

About two dozen German prisoners of war, guarded by two white American soldiers, entered the station. Trimmingham stood outside, watching in shock through the window. The enemy prisoners walked into the lunchroom, took tables, and were served right away. They ate and talked, laughed and smoked cigarettes.

"Are these men sworn enemies of this country? Why are they treated better than we are?" Trimmingham challenged. "If we are to die for our country, then why does the government allow such things to go on?"

Thurgood Marshall

No single lawyer could possibly handle the avalanche of abuses reported by African American soldiers and sailors. But Thurgood Marshall was willing to try.

Six foot two and slim, with a thin mustache, Marshall was the lead attorney for the National Association for the Advancement of Colored People (NAACP), an important civil rights organization based in New York City. Founded in 1909, the NAACP was dedicated to the struggle for equal rights and opportunities for African Americans. At just thirty-four, Thurgood Marshall was already known as one of the best civil rights lawyers in the country. When black servicemen needed help, Marshall was the man they turned to.

"I gave them someplace they could come," he later said. "If it got real rough, I'd be there."

The desk in Marshall's Manhattan office was cluttered with ever-growing piles of letters and articles describing stories like Trimmingham's—and worse. In late 1943, to take a typical example, a black army private named Rieves Bell was standing on a street corner in a Mississippi town, chatting with a couple of women. Four white civilians strode up.

One pushed Bell. He ignored it and went on talking with the women.

A second man shoved Bell, snarling, "Where'd you get that uniform?"

From Uncle Sam, Bell said.

"Take off that soldier suit."

Bell refused. Two of the men grabbed Bell, and the others began punching and kicking him. The police drove up and stopped the fight. The only man they arrested was Private Bell.

He was charged with assault, found guilty, and sentenced to three and a half years in prison.

When Thurgood Marshall heard of cases like these, he collected evidence and sent it to the War Department, demanding the government do more to protect its men in uniform. The response was always the same: segregation was a way of life in much of the country, and the federal government had no intention of interfering in local customs.

This enraged Marshall—but never discouraged him. Marshall saw his work as a fight for justice, and it was deeply personal.

Thurgood Marshall grew up in Baltimore, Maryland, where the schools, the parks, and even the stores were strictly segregated. There wasn't a place in all of downtown, Marshall remembered, where a black kid could use the bathroom.

At fifteen, he found an after-school job making deliveries for a clothing store. One afternoon he climbed onto a crowded trolley, holding a stack of hat boxes that rose over his head. Unable to see past the boxes, he bumped into the passenger in front of him.

A hand grabbed Marshall's shirt collar from behind and yanked him down the trolley steps.

"Don't push in front of a white lady!" the white man shouted.

"Damn it," Marshall barked back, "I'm just trying to get on the damned bus."

"Nigger, don't you talk to me like that!"

Marshall's mind raced to something his father told him often: "Anyone calls you a nigger, you not only got my permission to fight him—you got my *orders* to fight him."

The teenager dropped the hats and started swinging his

skinny arms in wild windmill punches. The man drove his head into Marshall's stomach, and the two fell to the sidewalk, tumbling and gouging. A policeman pushed through the gathering crowd and pulled the fighters apart. Only Marshall was arrested.

When his boss came down to the station to get him out, Marshall apologized for the ruined hats.

The elderly Jewish man put his arm around Marshall's shoulder and said, "It was worth it, if you're right."

After that Marshall never stopped fighting, though his teachers helped him find more effective tools than fists. Whenever he got in trouble in school, which, he confessed, was often, he was sent to the basement with a copy of the United States Constitution, and not let out until he memorized a passage. "Before I left that school I knew the whole thing by heart," Marshall said.

In those basement study sessions, Marshall was stunned to discover that the Constitution guaranteed the same basic rights to all Americans, regardless of race. Of particular interest was the Fourteenth Amendment, ratified in 1868, which specifically forbids states from denying any citizen "equal protection of the laws."

Segregation was not only immoral, Marshall realized, it was unconstitutional. He decided to become a lawyer and prove it in court.

Marshall worked sixteen-hour days during World War II, juggling cases from around the country. He spent most of his time on the road, traveling thousands of miles every month by train, bus, and car, living on adrenaline and too much junk food. With no office to work from, he'd fold his tall frame into the back of a car and tap out legal documents with his typewriter on his lap.

There was no end to the battles calling for Marshall's attention. He'd take on segregation laws in one town, and then defend falsely accused black prisoners somewhere else. He'd fight for voting rights one week, and the next challenge rules allowing states to pay black teachers less than whites.

And there was the long line of African American soldiers and sailors in need of help.

Lieutenant Nora Green, for example, was an Army nurse at the Tuskegee training base in Alabama. While shopping in nearby Montgomery, she got on a public bus, paid her fare, and sat. The driver told her to get off and wait outside while all the white passengers at the bus stop got on first.

Green refused to move. The driver cursed at her and called the police, who came and told her to get off the bus. She explained that she was due back on base for duty. The officers picked Green up, hit her, and dragged her to jail. She was let out the next morning—after paying a fine.

Green notified the NAACP, and the NAACP protested to the War Department and the Department of Justice. Rather than addressing the injustice, the government ordered Green to stop talking about the incident.

There were many similar cases, and some turned truly violent. Private Edward Green boarded a bus near his Louisiana base, and found a seat. The driver ordered Green to move back— he was sitting in a "white only" row. Green told the driver he'd sooner get off the bus than change seats. The bus stopped. The men exchanged hostile words as the soldier got off. The driver followed Green down the street, pulled out a pistol, and killed him.

The state declined to prosecute the driver. The Justice Department refused to investigate. The driver kept right on driving his route, with his murder weapon by his seat.

Stories like these didn't make the pages of mainstream newspapers, but they *were* reported in black newspapers. And all over the country—including at Port Chicago—black soldiers and sailors read the stories and wondered why the government was allowing such injustice to go unpunished.

"I hope you can realize the effect on the morale of the Negro soldiers," Marshall wrote to the Justice Department, protesting their lack of action in the Edward Green case. "Although one of their members is killed without provocation, the same government for which they are fighting refuses to take any action whatsoever to prosecute the guilty party."

Both civilian and military leaders hid behind the same old argument. Segregation was a fact of life, they said, and trying to force a change would upset white communities and white soldiers. "The urgency of the war situation does not justify experimentation," explained one general.

Marshall fought on. But he could feel the frustration and anger growing.

"Negro soldiers are damned tired of the treatment they are getting," reported a black army chaplain in 1944. "It grows out of the un-American treatment which plagues his every day, while at the same time having to listen to loud voices telling him what a great honor it is to die for his country."

"Things are slowly coming to a head," warned a black sailor from a base in Virginia. "All it needs is a little incident to light the fuse."

HOT CARGO

IN APRIL 1944, Captain Merrill T. Kinne took over command of Port Chicago. Kinne's job was to keep the ammunition moving from trains to ships as quickly as possible.

Kinne came into the job with the common prejudices against black sailors. "I have never felt that it would be possible to maintain a satisfactory loading rate with the type of enlisted personnel assigned to Port Chicago," he told his officers, "unless every officer in a supervisory capacity keeps continually in mind the necessity for getting this ammunition out."

Kinne's solution was to promote competition by posting the daily tonnage moved by each division on a chalkboard at the pier. Divisions loading the most were rewarded with free movies.

"It was as fast as you can go," Percy Robinson said of the pace of work. "It was a challenge."

"It was pressure," remembered Albert Williams. "It was a rush, rush."

An official Navy report would later declare: "Efforts were made by the officers to bring home to the men the necessity for care in the handling of explosives."

Percy Robinson (bending over) places boxes of ammunition onto a cargo net so that it can be loaded onto a ship.

But that was *after* the disaster, when the officers were scrambling to deflect blame from themselves. The men who did the work at Port Chicago told a very different story.

"We were pushed," said Joe Small. "The officers used to pit one division against the other. I often heard them argue over what division was beating the others."

Even more alarming to Small was when he realized Lieutenant Delucchi and other officers were actually placing bets on whose division could load the fastest.

"If he decided that he wanted to make $100," Small said of Delucchi, "and that we could outwork the Second Division,

then he would bet the commander of the Second Division that we would put on more tonnage than his division would."

If Small's division fell short, the men were left to deal with a very unhappy lieutenant.

"I think in the minds of a lot of people, including myself, what we were doing there was essential," Spencer Sikes later said of the vital job the Port Chicago men were doing. "The ammo had to be there. Somebody had to do it."

American troops needed massive quantities of ammunition,

and they needed it fast. The Port Chicago sailors appreciated this. What bothered them, more than the dangerous working conditions, was the feeling they'd been singled out for this work because of their race.

From the Navy's point of view, the sailors at Port Chicago were treated like any other enlisted men. All sailors had dangerous jobs, and there was no use whining about it. "There was no discrimination or any unusual treatment of these men," a Navy report insisted.

But naval leaders were ignoring one essential point—segregation *was* discrimination. The very fact that black sailors were stuck at Port Chicago instead of being allowed to fight *was* discrimination. And the black sailors felt it, even if the white officers didn't.

"We used to talk about what big fools we were, you know, only black boys loading ammunition," Martin Bordenave remembered. "Only white boys can go aboard ships."

"You didn't see no white boys out there loading," said another sailor, Willie Gay. "I guess they figured that was all we were good for."

The loading continued in three shifts, around the clock. As the speed of the work increased, so did the tension at the waterfront.

Cyril Sheppard described rolling huge bombs into one of the nets on the pier. The winch operator lifted the net too quickly and the heavy load swung back—*CRACK!*—into the side of the railroad car.

"Damn, man!" Sheppard shouted. "Can't you do better than that?"

Sailors prepare to receive a load of crates on board an ammunition ship.

"Oh, man, don't worry about that," the winch operator said. Like many on the pier, he coped with the danger by trying to pretend it didn't exist.

On another day, Percy Robinson was standing on a stack of ammunition in the hold of a ship tied to the pier. Nets were lowering bombs into the hold, and the men were stacking them higher and higher.

As one bomb came down it slipped from the tilting net and slammed, nose first, into the side of the ship. Everyone froze.

A *PSSSSSSSSSSS*-sound filled the hold. Some sort of red liquid started shooting out the front of the bomb.

Men dove for the ladders leading up to deck.

"You had ten, twelve guys trying to get out of the hold at the same time," Robinson remembered. "You can't do it. Some guys broke their legs trying to get out of that hold."

As the terrified crew stumbled and limped and collapsed onto the pier, they noticed the other crews were just standing there, calmly looking on. Some of the men were laughing.

It was just dye, someone on the pier explained. The bombs had pressurized capsules of dye in their noses, different colors for different ships, and when one of the bombs hit something, the dye would spray out. That way, even in the chaos of battle, crews could see where their bombs were exploding, and adjust their aim.

It all made perfect sense—except that no one had bothered to inform the men loading the bombs.

"They should have told us about that," Robinson said after this senseless accident. "We should have gone to school or something to learn about something like this."

Most of the young sailors were afraid to gripe to the officers about the increasingly dangerous working conditions. The quick-tempered Lieutenant Delucchi, in particular, was not an easy man to approach.

Not surprisingly, Joe Small was one of the few to speak up. During one hectic shift, Delucchi came over to check on the progress.

"How are things going?" he asked Small.

"Rough," Small said. "I think we're pushing too hard."

Delucchi looked at his watch. He asked Small if he thought the men could load thirty tons by the end of the shift.

"Sure, if the place doesn't blow up," Small said. "And someday it will."

Delucchi had heard this worry before. He responded the way he always did.

"If it does," he told Small, grinning, "neither you nor I will be around to know about it."

By July 1944, there were 1,431 black enlisted men at Port Chicago, and 71 white officers. The base was guarded by 106 marines, all white.

"The 17th of July was a beautiful day," Robert Routh would recall many years later. "It was a Monday, a hot July day, and for some reason I felt a great foreboding, and I don't know why."

At the pier, crews were loading the cargo ship *E. A. Bryan.* The *Bryan* was scheduled to take on 8,500 tons of bombs and ammunition; about half of that was already aboard.

That afternoon a civilian plumber from Pittsburg named Albert Carr drove down to the waterfront. He'd gotten a call that the steam-powered brakes on one of the winches were malfunctioning.

As Carr replaced a faulty part in the winch, the rapid loading continued around him. He heard bombs rolling down ramps from the boxcars, clinking together on the pier. A sailor walking past him lost his grip on a shell, and it fell with a heavy thud.

Carr announced that he was done, and the winch operator climbed on to test the brakes. They were working fine. Seeing this, the plumber quickly began gathering his tools.

"Where are you going?" an officer asked.

"Well, I'm through," Carr said. "I don't like the looks of things around here."

The plumber headed back to Pittsburg as fast as he could.

Joe Small and the men of Division Four finished work at three o'clock that afternoon. They rode the cattle cars back to their barracks as fresh crews took over the loading.

For Spencer Sikes, it was a liberty day. He was hanging around the base when he heard someone shouting:

"Sikes! Telephone!"

He picked up the phone, and was surprised when the woman on the other end introduced herself as the mother of Alverta, a girl he'd met recently in Berkeley.

"Spence, what are you doing today?" asked the mother.

"Nothing, I'm off today."

"Why don't you come into town tonight? Why don't you guys go to a movie?"

Sounded a lot better than reading in his bunk. "Yes," he said, "that's a good idea."

He showered and shaved and walked to the bus stop.

"That date really saved my life," he later said.

Spencer Sikes

At 6 p.m., as Sikes headed for Berkeley, a second ship, the *Quin-alt Victory*, cruised up to Port Chicago and was tied up across the pier from the *E. A. Bryan*. While Division Three continued moving explosives onto the *Bryan*, the men of Division Six climbed onto the *Quinalt Victory* to prepare its holds for loading.

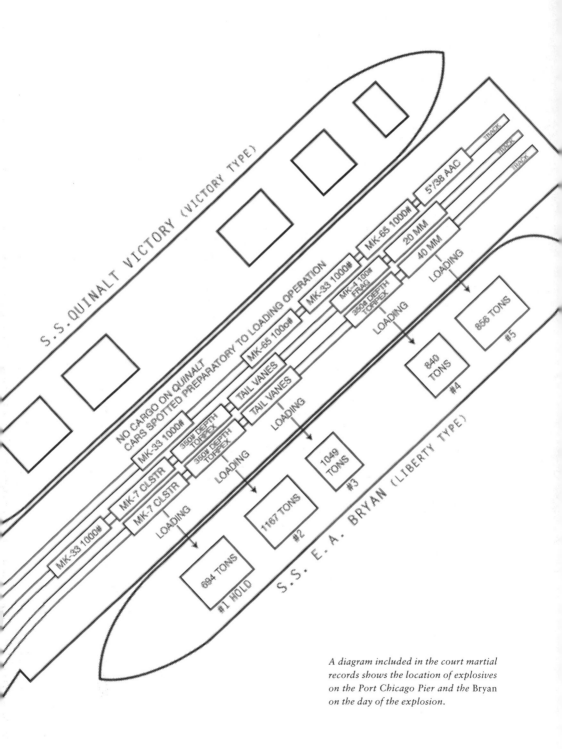

A diagram included in the court martial records shows the location of explosives on the Port Chicago Pier and the Bryan on the day of the explosion.

The air cooled quickly as the sun set. The floodlights on the pier came on. Sixteen railroad boxcars, holding about 430 tons of bombs and ammunition, were lined up on pier. Armed marines patrolled the waterfront. Coast Guard boats patrolled the bay.

A little after 9 p.m., several crew members of the *Quinault Victory* left the ship for a few hours of liberty. Most of the crew stayed aboard.

Lieutenant Commander Glen Ringquist paced the pier, supervising the work. The holds of the *Bryan* were loaded nearly to their tops. As Ringquist watched, sailors added what they called the "hot cargo"—incendiary bombs with fuses already attached. Ringquist saw that the men were handling these bombs very carefully.

"Operations were proceeding in a normal routine matter," Ringquist would later report. "Conditions normal about this time."

At 9:30, Captain Kinne came down for a look at the work. Seeing that everything was going well, he got back in his jeep and drove to the officers' quarters. In the enlisted men's barracks, a mile from the pier, men were getting ready for lights out.

"I had pimples, you know, still being a teenager," Robert Routh remembered. Routh spread acne cream on his cheeks, put his gear away, said his prayers, and got into bed.

At 10 p.m. exactly, the usual announcement came over speakers: "Lights out, quiet about the deck."

Men settled into their bunks.

Joe Small lay on his top bunk in the dark, thinking fondly of a woman he'd met in Pittsburg. They had a date to meet again the next night.

"But naturally that never came about," Small later said. "See, everything changed."

THE EXPLOSION

JOE SMALL WAS STILL AWAKE AT 10:18 P.M.

He was lying on his stomach when he heard what sounded like a thunderclap coming from the direction of the pier.

"Oh my God, we're being bombed!" someone shouted.

Men lifted their heads from their pillows and looked out the windows in the direction of the sound. Then, just seconds after the first blast, came a much more massive explosion.

"The sky lit up, and it's just like the sun rose," Percy Robinson remembered.

"All these tremendous beautiful flashes in the sky," said Robert Routh, "like at a Fourth of July celebration."

The speeding shock wave slammed into the barracks.

"It was like someone shot in the windows with a shotgun," Willie Gay said.

Flying glass slashed many of the men. "My left arm got mutilated," Robinson said, "face, head, neck, shoulders."

Routh, who was looking out toward the pier, took glass shards in both eyes.

The blast lifted Small straight into the air, his mattress still underneath him. Flipping over as he fell, he landed facedown on the barracks floor, with the mattress on top of him—lucky protection from the shower of glass and wood splinters.

Cyril Sheppard, who'd been sitting on the toilet reading a letter from home, was knocked across the bathroom and into the wall. He got up and dashed out into the dark barracks.

"Men were screaming," he remembered. "Glass was flying all over the place. The whole building was caving in."

"First thing I thought—Pearl Harbor again," Albert Williams said. "That's what it was like, somebody dropped bombs over the place."

As he lay bleeding in the dark, Robinson heard a series of sharp cracks. The wood beams holding up the second story were giving way.

"Get out of the barracks!" men shouted. "It's coming down!"

Crawling, tripping, carrying each other, the men raced outside as the building tilted over.

Unable to see from his wounded eyes, Routh called out, "Hey! Come and get me and take me to the sick bay!"

Someone shouted back, "The sick bay has been blown up!"

Lieutenant Commander Glen Ringquist had a closer look at the blast than the men in the barracks.

He had left the pier at 10:15 p.m., just three minutes before the explosion. He was in his jeep, driving away from the waterfront, when the sky lit up. Ringquist jumped out of the car and watched a column of smoke and red flames shooting thousands of feet into the air.

"And then darkness set in," Ringquist said, "and fragments started to fall."

Fiery hot chunks of metal, some over 100 pounds, rained down all over the base.

An Air Force pilot cruising above Suisun Bay witnessed the blast from 9,000 feet above. "It seemed to me that there was a huge ring of fire, spread out on all sides," he later reported. "And there were pieces of metal that were white and orange in color, hot, that went a ways above us. They were quite large."

The movie theater in the town of Port Chicago, about a mile from the base, was showing a war film. A bombing scene had just begun, causing some to think the loud boom they heard was part of the picture—until the side wall of the theater buckled and pieces of the roof started falling in. The panicked audience darted into the street in time to see the flames rising above the Port Chicago pier.

In a café next to the theater, Morris Rich and another sailor

Sailors look out through barracks windows that were blown out in the blast.

on liberty from the *Quinalt Victory* had just ordered sandwiches. They never got them.

"We hadn't been sitting there maybe five minutes or less and this explosion took place," Rich remembered. "We found ourselves across the room. I mean, it blew us out of the booth clear across the room."

Rich stumbled into the street and stood, amid raining hunks of steel, looking down toward the pier. He knew instantly that everyone on his ship was dead.

The massive blast was felt all over the Bay Area. In Berkeley, thirty miles from Port Chicago, seismographs recorded a jolt with the force of a small earthquake.

Spencer Sikes and his date, Alverta, were sitting in a Berkeley movie theater when they heard the boom and felt the building shake. Moments later a theater employee ran out to pass on an announcement he'd just heard on the radio: "All military personnel stationed at Port Chicago, please report back immediately!"

Sikes dropped Alverta at home and jumped on a bus.

Back at the base, Captain Kinne ran out of the officers' quarters and looked toward the water.

"What happened?" someone shouted to him.

"I don't know," he said. "I think the ships blew up."

Kinne saw that falling debris had ignited grass fires, and flames were spreading toward several boxcars full of ammunition. A team of enlisted men and officers were working together to put out the fires, and they seemed to have things under control.

"There was no appearance of panic or disorder," Kinne would later report with pride.

Outside of the barracks, quick-thinking sailors had flipped on truck headlights. Crouching in the beams of light, men with only minor scrapes treated the more seriously wounded.

"Fellows were cut and bleeding all over the place," Joe Small recalled. "One fellow's feet were bleeding and I gave him my shoes. Another fellow had a cut all the way down his arm, and I put a tourniquet on it to try to stop the bleeding. There were no medics around—it was chaos."

Another group of sailors formed a crew of volunteers to head down to the pier. Percy Robinson, still unaware of how badly cut up he was, stepped forward.

"I want to volunteer," he said to his squad leader.

The guy turned to him and asked, "Hey, did you see Percy get out of the barracks?"

"*I'm* Percy, I'm going down to the docks."

The squad leader looked more closely at Robinson's blood-streaked face, and recognized him.

"You can't go," he said. "You have to go to the hospital to get sewed up."

Cyril Sheppard was among the sailors who jumped into a truck and sped toward the water. But when they got near the pier, the driver stopped.

"Go on down!" guys in the back of the truck shouted. "What the hell are you staying up here for?"

"Can't go no further," the driver said, pointing out at the bay.

Everyone stood up and looked.

The pier was gone. The ships were gone. The truck lights shone out on an empty patch of water. Low waves lapped at the shore.

"Just calm and peaceful," Sheppard recalled. "I didn't even see any smoke."

THE INQUIRY

LATER THAT NIGHT, in the hospital, a doctor removed Robert Routh's left eye. "And the right eye was lacerated," Routh later said, "and so consequently, I lost the sight in that too."

Spencer Sikes made it back to Port Chicago a few hours after the blast. Out of curiosity, he took a quick look at his bunk—and saw sword-sized glass slivers piercing his pillow, buried deep into the mattress below. If he'd been in bed at the time of the blast, he knew, he'd be dead.

It was not until sunrise that the men at Port Chicago got a clear look at the scene of devastation. The huge open space leading down to the water was dotted with piles of rubble, burned grass, splintered wood. One 200-pound chunk of gray steel—part of one of the ships, clearly—lay more than two miles from the pier.

The men walked along the railroad tracks leading down to the bay. At the waterfront, where the pier used to be, two twisted rails stuck out a few feet from the shore and ended in the air above the water.

The 1,200-foot pier was simply gone. The locomotive and

Onlookers gather on what remains of the pier at Port Chicago to survey the damage.

The stern of the Quinalt Victory *juts from the bay following the explosion.*

ammunition boxcars that had been on the pier at the time of the blast had disintegrated. The only piece of the *Quinalt Victory* in sight was its upright stern, sticking up from the water just off-shore. Of the *E. A. Bryan*, which had been packed with nearly ten million pounds of explosives, nothing visible remained. The ship had essentially exploded like one gigantic bomb—one of the biggest man-made explosions in history to that point.

Shreds of clothing and other bits of debris bobbed on the water. Some of the men with only minor injuries were given the gory task of wading into the bay to pull out bodies, and parts of bodies.

"Man, it was awful," Jack Crittenden remembered. "You'd see a head floating across the water—just the head—or an arm."

"Very seldom you'd find a whole body," DeWitt Jameson said. "You may find a shoe with a foot in it. Half a head blown off, or something like that. We had to do this for a couple of days, until the authorities felt that we had found everybody that we were going to find."

Of the human remains pulled from the bay, only fifty-one bodies were whole enough to identify. There had been more than 300 people at the waterfront at the time of the blast.

EXTRA — The Shreveport

SHREVEPORT, LOUISIANA—TUESDAY, JULY 18, 1944

VOL. LXXII—NO. 48

650 REPORTED DEAD

EXPLOSION ON C

A headline that ran in the Shreveport Times *on the day following the Port Chicago blast estimated the death toll at 650. The count was later confirmed to be 320.*

★ ★ ★

The morning after the explosion, the Navy let reporters into Port Chicago. The blast was already headline news all over the country.

"As we walked down the streets, we stepped over broken glass, pieces of steel from the exploded ships and debris of all sorts," wrote one reporter. "On either side were shattered barracks with gaping holes, as though hit by shells. From their windows, shades flapped miserably in the wind."

Captain Nelson Goss held a brief press conference to discuss the known facts.

Every single person aboard the two ships, and everyone on the pier, had been instantly killed. A total of 320 men were dead, 202 of them black sailors who'd been loading ammunition. Another 390 men, mostly sailors in the barracks, were injured.

A reporter asked if they could have a look at the blast site.

No, Goss said. "We wouldn't want to go there anyway. It is a terrible thing and not anything you want to write about."

Someone asked about the cause of the explosion.

"We have no basis for giving any cause," Goss said, "as there are no close survivors to give evidence of what happened."

In his own statement to the press, Admiral Carleton Wright, one of the Navy's top officials on the West Coast, spoke of the vital contribution the victims had made to the war effort. "Their sacrifice could not have been greater had it occurred on a battleship or a beachhead on the war fronts."

Wright also praised the men of Port Chicago for fighting fires and aiding the wounded in the hectic hours after the blast. "As was to be expected, Negro personnel attached to the Naval Magazine Port Chicago performed bravely and efficiently in the emergency," he told the papers. "As real Navy men, they simply carried on in the crisis attendant on the explosion in accordance with our Service's highest traditions."

On July 21, four days after the explosion, the Navy convened an official court of inquiry to try to determine the cause of the disaster. One major challenge quickly became apparent—there were no living witnesses. Anyone close enough to have seen how the blast began was dead.

Based on the descriptions of witnesses who were a mile or more away, it was clear there had been two separate explosions. First a smaller one, then, about six seconds later, the massive blast that flattened the base. The smaller explosion must have sparked the bigger one. But what caused the smaller one?

This brought up the issue of the way explosives were being handled. Some of the younger officers testified about Captain Kinne's policy of posting tonnage figures, which encouraged

competition between divisions. Kinne insisted this had absolutely no impact on safety at the pier.

The Navy, in reporting its findings, agreed. "The posting of the amounts loaded by each division did not operate to increase the hazards of loading," the report concluded. "Unsafe practices and speed at the expense of safety were not permitted by anyone in authority."

The real problem, insisted many of the officers, was the black sailors.

"The consensus of opinion of the witnesses," summarized the official report, "is that the colored enlisted personnel are neither temperamentally nor intellectually capable of handling high explosives. . . . It is an admitted fact, supported by the testimony of the witnesses, that there was rough and careless handling of the explosives being loaded aboard ships at Port Chicago."

When the report used the word *witnesses*, it was referring exclusively to white officers. Surviving black sailors who had done the loading didn't have a chance to tell their stories or offer their own opinions. The court never asked them to testify.

While the Navy began clearing the rubble from Port Chicago, the black sailors were transferred to a nearby base, Camp Shoemaker. The men were not told when they would be put back to work, or what type of work they would be doing.

"We had no idea what was happening," Joe Small remembered.

Sitting around in the barracks day after idle day, the men talked of the friends they would never see again. "You knew all

Automobiles parked near the Port Chicago pier were demolished by the blast.

of these people that got killed," said Spencer Sikes. "There was a mourning period."

They traded theories about the cause of the explosion. Percy Robinson, his face and arm wrapped in bandages, was convinced there had been some kind of accident, probably involving the "hot cargo" incendiary bombs.

Several others suspected sabotage—they believed an enemy had snuck on base and somehow triggered the blast.

"I just don't believe that it was sabotage," Freddie Meeks argued. "I believe it came from an explosion in one of them boxcars."

Freddie Meeks

With nothing to do but wait and think and wonder, the men's already frayed nerves stretched toward the snapping point.

"Everybody was scared," Robinson remembered. "If somebody dropped a box or slammed a door, people began jumping around like crazy."

One of the men near Joe Small's bunk dealt with the fear by making a joke of it. In the middle of the night, he tiptoed to the light switch, flipped on the lights, and yelled, "Fire!"

During another quiet moment in the barracks, Small watched the same guy lift a stiff corner of his bedsheet and jam it into the whirling blades of a fan.

"It made a '*R R R R R*' noise," Small recalled. "And there was a spontaneous explosion toward that back door." The men ripped the door off the hinges as they dove out of the building.

As usual, Small was the one to take the men's concerns to the officers. "I requested that he be moved out of our barracks," Small explained. "They moved him out."

In Washington, D.C., Congress began considering a bill to compensate the victims of the Port Chicago disaster. As it was first written, the legislation allowed residents of the town of Port Chicago and families of dead servicemen to receive grants of up to $5,000. But John Rankin, a rabidly pro-segregationist House member from Mississippi, objected on the grounds that many of the families getting money would be black.

Congress reduced the maximum compensation to $3,000.

In an editorial titled "Port Chicago Heroes," the *Pittsburgh Courier* blasted back at the continuing discrimination against black servicemen. "What did they die for?" the paper asked of the Port Chicago victims. "Why did these heroes risk death?"

A memorial service for the victims of the Port Chicago explosion was held on July 30, 1944.

America was battling for its freedom and way of life in this war, and black servicemen and women were part of the world-wide fight. "Negro Americans rallied even though they knew that the American way for them was something different, and something less, from what it is for the white American."

Now, two and a half years into World War II, more than 200 black sailors had died in service at the segregated base of Port Chicago. "Ought not this sacrifice," the paper asked, "touch the conscience of America? Is one to assume, as the nation continues to ask the Negro to die for less than the white American dies, that the national conscience of America is at such a low moral level that most Americans are satisfied that the blood of Negroes is worth less than that of whites?

"At some time, every Negro in the armed services asks himself what he is getting for the supreme sacrifice he is called upon to make."

Letters continued to pour into Thurgood Marshall's New York City office.

In an all-too-typical case, a black army private named Purdie Jackson was severely beaten for refusing to leave the "white only" section of a Nashville, Tennessee, drugstore. The army charged Jackson with assault, court-martialed him, and gave him twelve years in prison. Marshall prepared an appeal on Jackson's behalf.

Other soldiers and sailors wrote to Marshall describing how they'd been dishonorably discharged from the military for speaking out against racist treatment. Marshall and his three-lawyer staff took on as many of the cases as they could.

It was frustrating work, but Marshall cautioned fellow African Americans against turning bitter or losing hope. As rough as things were in the United States, he argued, they'd be a lot worse under the dictators America was fighting in World War II. The challenge ahead, as Marshall saw it, was to help win the war *and* to continue pressuring the country to confront segregation.

"We must not be delayed by people who say 'the time is not ripe,'" Marshall told the crowd at an NAACP conference in July 1944. "Persons who deny to us our civil rights should be brought to justice now. Many people believe the time is always 'ripe' to discriminate against Negroes. All right then—the time is always 'ripe' to bring them to justice."

What Marshall could not have known was that he was about to get a chance to take the fight for justice directly to the United States Navy.

★ ★ ★

At the beginning of August, Joe Small and the other Port Chicago men were moved to Mare Island Naval Shipyard, a base on San Pablo Bay, in the city of Vallejo. They still didn't know what the Navy had planned for them. But ships were being loaded with ammunition at Mare Island. That gave them a pretty good idea.

"The only thing we knew was handling ammunition," Small later said, "and we fully expected to be asked to go back to the same work."

They'd have preferred any other assignment.

"Put me on a ship and let me fight out there, take my chances there," one sailor said. "Why lose your life on somebody else's negligence?"

At some point during that first week of August, a list circulated through the barracks, and many of the men signed it. The sailors later said it was a petition requesting a transfer to some other type of duty. The Navy would insist it was a list of people who intended to refuse to load ammunition. We'll never know, because the list disappeared.

"I was instrumental in having it destroyed," Small explained years later. Some serious decisions were coming up, he knew, and it was best to put nothing in writing. "When you put your name on a list, then you become a supporting part of whatever that list stands for," Small explained. "And there's very little chance of your changing your mind even if you wanted to."

On August 8, the men of Small's division were issued new work gloves—the same types of gloves they had used on the pier at Port Chicago.

"If these are for handling ammunition," joked one of the sailors, "I never touch the stuff."

But he took the gloves. They all did.

The Navy would later charge that the sailors held a secret meeting in their barracks that night. According to the men, there was nothing secret about it. Given everything that had happened, of course they sat up discussing the orders they were likely to get the next day—and how they were going to respond.

"What you gonna do?" someone asked Cyril Sheppard.

"I know what I'm gonna do," he said. "I ain't going."

As usual, the men wanted to know what Joe Small was thinking.

Actually, he hadn't yet made up his mind. Small knew he was being treated unfairly by the Navy, but did that give him the right to disobey orders? He was terrified of another explosion, but didn't sailors in combat zones face conditions at least as perilous? For Small, fear alone was insufficient cause for demanding different work. Besides, if it was dangerous to go back to work, there was also risk in refusing—could low-ranking sailors really defy the U.S. Navy without expecting serious consequences?

There were no easy answers. But the more Small considered his options, the clearer his decision became. "I was a winch operator," he remembered of his job at Port Chicago, "and I missed killing a man on the average of once a day. And it was all because of rushing, speed.

"I realized that I had to work. I wasn't trying to shirk work. But to go back to work under the same conditions with no improvements, no changes, the same group of officers that we had . . .

"So I came to the conclusion that I was not going back to the same work under the same conditions, under the same men. And that was it."

COLUMN LEFT

THE NEXT DAY, AUGUST 9, 1944, the men of Joe Small's division were sent to lunch early. At 11:15 a.m., Lieutenant Delucchi stepped into a small office on the base and picked up a microphone.

"Division Four, turn to for work," he announced into the mic.

Delucchi then walked toward Barracks C, where his men were quartered. As he crossed the base, he could see down to the pier on the opposite side of a narrow river. Docked at the pier was the USS *Sangay*, a large, empty ammunition ship.

As Delucchi strolled up to the barracks, the sailors, in their dungarees and blue work shirts, were coming out of the building. Many of the men still wore bandages on their arms and faces from the explosion. They lined up slowly—too slowly for the lieutenant.

"There was a bit of milling around," Delucchi later said. He stepped up to his chief petty officer, Elmer Boyer, and told Boyer to hurry the men into formation.

Sailors from other divisions stood outside the barracks,

The USS Wadleigh *docked for loading at the Mare Island Navy Yard in 1945.*

chatting and smoking cigarettes. It's possible they were out there simply because there was no smoking allowed inside the barracks. Or maybe they suspected something interesting was about to happen, and wanted to watch.

"Okay, move 'em out," Delucchi ordered Boyer when the men were ready.

"Right face!" shouted Boyer. "Forward march!"

The division marched in ranks toward the river. As always, Joe Small marched on the left side of the men, calling cadence.

The group soon approached a T-shaped turn in the road. The path to the right led to the parade ground. The path to the left led down to the ferry, which crossed the river to the loading dock.

A turn to the right meant another day of routine exercise. A turn to the left meant loading ammunition.

"Column left," Delucchi ordered Boyer.

"Column left!" Boyer shouted.

And then came one of those seemingly small moments that winds up changing the course of history.

Someone in the ranks stopped. Or maybe many of the men stopped at once—different men remembered it differently. Either way, the marching sailors banged together and came to a stop in the road.

Men were looking around. Some seemed confused.

Delucchi turned to his division.

"Will you go back to work?" he demanded, stepping toward them.

No one answered.

"You're going to load this ship," he told the men, pointing across the water.

Percy Robinson heard someone near him mutter, "Oh no we ain't. We're not gonna go."

"Joseph Small!" Delucchi shouted. "Front and center!"

Small marched to the front of the formation, turned, and stood face-to-face with the lieutenant.

"Small, will you return to duty?"

"No, sir," said Small.

Delucchi glared at Small: "Is that final?"

"Yes, sir, that's final."

Someone back in the ranks called out: "If Small don't go, we won't go either!"

Delucchi's face flushed blood red. He spun away from Small and marched off, leaving his division at the T in the road.

The men watched Delucchi walk to the administration building where, they knew, he would report to his superiors. They waited. Some sat on the grass.

About fifteen minutes later, a chaplain named Jefferson Flowers left the administration building and walked up to the group. He asked them to gather around.

"What's the trouble?" asked Flowers.

A few men spoke up, saying they didn't want to load ammunition.

Flowers tried to persuade them to get on the ferry to the loading dock. It was their duty, he explained. "They said that they would obey any other order," Flowers would later testify, "but they would not handle ammunition."

"We told him he was wasting his time talking to us," remembered Willie Gay. "He should let the white boys load the ammunition."

The chaplain tried another approach, reminding the men that other sailors and soldiers faced enemy fire on ships and in foxholes—they couldn't just stop in the middle because they were afraid. Flowers saw tears in the eyes of some of the men as they considered this.

"You can fight back in foxholes," someone called out, "but you can't fight back here."

Delucchi returned. He marched the men to the parade ground, and stepped up onto the reviewing stand.

"You men have given me a hell of a letdown," Delucchi told his division. "You took an oath, like I did, to obey orders."

He told them he'd thought they were man enough to handle things when the going got hot, but evidently he'd been mistaken. What's more, he said, the men were letting down black leaders around the nation, and their entire race.

"There are a lot of people who're working for the Negro people," Delucchi lectured, "and it won't help the Negro people any if these people withdraw their support when they find out about how you men are acting."

Delucchi was still talking when the executive officer of the base, Commander Joseph Tobin, sped up in a jeep. He told Delucchi he wanted to speak to the sailors individually and ordered the lieutenant to march his division to the recreation building. The men took seats in the auditorium, and waited their turn, as Tobin called them into his office one by one.

"You have been ordered by your division officer, while in formation, to report to work at the ammunition depot," Commander Tobin told each man. "You refused to obey this order. I am now ordering you, individually and personally, as commanding officer, to report for work immediately."

A few of the men agreed. They marched down toward the water to wait for the ferry.

Joe Small, Percy Robinson, and most of the others refused to go.

Tobin warned them of the grave consequences of disobeying

orders in time of war. They would probably end up facing a court-martial, he threatened.

Many told Tobin they would obey any order—except the order to handle ammunition.

Tobin angrily explained that in the Navy it wasn't up to an individual sailor to decide which orders to follow.

After leaving Tobin's office, each man who refused to return to work was marched outside to a nearby baseball field. Armed marines stood around the field, guarding the growing group.

Standing on the field, Percy Robinson watched the men of his division gather in twos and threes, talking quietly. Like many of the men, Robinson began thinking about what he had just done, and why.

"You know, all this stuff builds up," he said later, explaining his mindset at this critical moment. "A lot of things you didn't like before, you just didn't do anything about 'em. But now they're all piled up. I guess you put 'em all together."

"I felt like I was being mistreated," he added. "I had no other recourse to fight back but to refuse to go back to work."

Meanwhile, there was more trouble on the base.

At 1:30 that afternoon, Lieutenant Carleton Morehouse mustered Division Eight in front of Barracks C. When the 104 men were lined up, he told them the division's orders were to take the ferry across the water and load ammunition on the *Sangay*.

Many of these men had watched Division Four stop in the road two hours earlier. Now it was their turn to decide.

"I order you to load ammunition with me," Morehouse told

his division. "All who are willing to load with me stand fast. Any who refuse to obey this order, fall out."

Many of the men began stepping out of the ranks. In the confusion, Morehouse couldn't tell who was willing to load and who wasn't. One by one, he ordered each man in the division to step forward.

"I order you to load ammunition with me," Morehouse said. "Think before you answer, because a refusal means severe disciplinary action. Will you load ship with me, yes or no?"

Eight men said yes. Ninety-six said no.

Half an hour later, Lieutenant James Tobin (no relation to the executive officer) called Division Two together. Like the other divisions, they were scheduled to begin loading the *Sangay*.

"Many men from the other divisions have refused to obey orders," Tobin told his men. "Refusal to obey orders in time of war may have very serious consequences. I know some of you men may be afraid, but that is no reason for disobeying orders."

Then Tobin got to the point. "I am ordering you men to turn to for your regularly assigned duty of loading ship. Men who obey that order, stand fast. Men who refuse to obey that order, move on to one side."

A large group of men stepped to the side.

Tobin addressed these men. "I order you to turn to for your regularly assigned duty of loading ship," he said. "If you obey that order, step to the rear. If not, give your name to Lieutenant Clement."

Some turned and walked right to Clement, who was writing names down on a clipboard. Others hesitated.

"Anthony, how about it?" Tobin said to a sailor named Douglas Anthony, who seemed undecided. "Are you going to obey orders or disobey orders?"

Anthony said he had no intention of disobeying orders, but he was afraid to load bombs.

"Get on the other side," Tobin said, pointing to Clement.

"How about you, McPherson?" Tobin asked, moving down the line.

"Frankly speaking, Mr. Tobin, I am afraid," Alphonso McPherson said.

"Give Lieutenant Clement your name, and go over there with the cowards."

Tobin pointed to Jack Crittenden. "Jack, now you're a fine young person, and no use getting yourself involved. Now come sign this saying you're going back to work."

"Lieutenant Tobin, I'm afraid," Crittenden said. "I got a chance over there with the enemy. But I ain't got a chance in that hold."

"Are you going to sign?" Tobin demanded.

"I'm afraid."

"When you say you're afraid, that means you refuse?"

"No, when I say I'm afraid, that means I'm afraid."

"That means you're refusing an order."

"No, that means I'm afraid."

Tobin pointed Crittenden toward Lieutenant Clement. Just twenty-six of Tobin's men agreed to load. Eighty-seven did not.

Of the 328 sailors in the three divisions scheduled to load ammunition that day, a total of 258 had refused. These men were told to go to the barracks and pack up their gear. Then they were marched, under guard, down to the river, where a barge was tied to the pier.

As the men crowded onto the large, flat boat, Lieutenant

Delucchi pulled Joe Small aside and they had a very short conversation. The details of exactly what was said would become a major point of contention between the two. But the gist of the talk, both agreed, was that Delucchi wanted Small to help see that the men of Division Four behaved themselves and followed orders on the barge.

Then Small walked onto the floating prison.

PRISON BARGE

"**WE WERE PACKED IN** like sardines," Joe Small later said of conditions on the prison barge.

"We were all scared," Jack Crittenden remembered, "and we didn't know what was going on."

At mealtimes, the prisoners were marched from the barge to the chow hall on base. At all other times, they remained on the barge, with marines watching from the pier. The main topic of conversation among the men was whether to give in and go back to loading ammunition.

"Two men would get to fighting right there on the barge," Small recalled, "because one thought that he should go back to duty and another thought he shouldn't."

One young sailor, just seventeen, pulled Small aside and quietly confessed he wanted to go back to work.

"You can," Small responded, "but I wouldn't advise it." The men were in this mess together, Small said, and they should see it through together. "If we go back as a unit, then that's one thing," he said. "But if we go back one at a time, the one that goes back will be looked down on by the others as a traitor."

The young man agreed to stay.

A day passed, and then another—still no word from the officers about what was going to happen next. Small could see the men on the crowded barge becoming increasingly tense. For many, the anger they'd long felt at the unfair conditions they faced in the Navy was now bubbling to the surface.

"There's no rule that says we have to march in ranks to go to chow," one of the sailors grumbled. "We can just walk."

"I'm not gonna march in cadence no more," another added.

"I'm with you."

"Look, man," someone else cut in, "you're in the Navy, and you got to abide by Navy rules."

At meals, Small noticed a few of the men slipping spoons or forks into their pockets and sneaking them back onto the barge. "I saw spoons made into knives, forks made into knives," he later said.

The marines on the pier warned the prisoners that they didn't want to have to fire into the crowded barge—but they would.

"Now, the slightest provocation, we will shoot."

"It was a pretty hairy situation," Small remembered, "and I got into it to try to offset a disaster that I saw coming."

On the second night on the barge, Small huddled with a few other men that the young sailors looked to as leaders. They agreed it was time to call a meeting. The word spread quickly and nearly everyone jammed together, with Small standing in the center of the crowd.

"All right fellows, listen to what is to be said," Small shouted. "It's as much for your good as it is for mine."

A confrontation with the guards would be bloody and disastrous, Small told the men. Besides acting defiantly and disorderly was just playing into the officers' hands.

"That is just what the officers want us to do; they want us to mess up," Small said. "The officers want us to do something, so they will have something on us. If we obey the shore patrol and the officers and don't get into trouble, they can't do anything to us."

Small hammered the point again, in stronger language. "We've got the officers by the balls," he said. "They can do nothing to us if we don't do anything to them. If we stick together, they can't do anything to us."

Some of the men clapped when Small was finished. The whole speech had lasted less than four minutes. At the time, Small thought no more about it. The mood was calmer after the meeting. The men obeyed orders and had no trouble with the guards.

On the barge, the talk turned to questions about the future. What would happen to the men if they kept refusing to load? Some thought the Navy would just transfer them to other duties. Some figured they'd get dishonorable discharges; some expected to be imprisoned. But talk about giving in had died down.

"We were stubborn," remembered Percy Robinson. "We were stuck, you know. We made a commitment. There was a few guys, a very few, wanted to change their minds, but most of the people were clear—they can't shove us around like this."

Small was determined to stick it out too. "Improve working conditions, this is what I, personally, was after," he later said. "And desegregation of the base."

★ ★ ★

On August 11, the third day on the barge, Small noticed Lieutenant Delucchi and a few other officers walking along the pier toward the barge.

"Something's up," he said.

Sure enough, the lieutenants all called for their divisions to step off the barge and fall into ranks. The men were marched from the pier to a nearby baseball field. The three divisions assembled in a U-shaped formation on the infield. Marines stood around the field, holding machine guns.

A jeep drove up and an officer in his early fifties jumped out and strode to the front of the formation.

"Just in case you don't know who I am," the man began, "my name is Admiral Wright, and I am the commandant of the Twelfth Naval District."

Admiral Carleton Wright paced along the rows of prisoners as he spoke.

"They tell me that some of you men want to go to sea. I believe that's a goddamn lie! I don't believe any of you have enough guts to go to sea!"

Wright leaned forward as he paced, and as he shouted the men could smell his lunch on his breath. Percy Robinson wished he could say something,

Admiral Carleton Wright

explain his actions, defend himself. "But what you going to do?" he told himself. "You stand still and you take the stuff."

"I handled ammunition for approximately thirty years, and I'm still here," Wright told the men. "I have a healthy respect for ammunition—anybody who doesn't is crazy. But I want to remind you men that mutinous conduct in time of war carries the death sentence, and the hazards of facing a firing squad are far greater than the hazards of handling ammunition."

The prisoners were stunned. This was the first they'd heard about mutiny or death sentences.

Wright wanted to be absolutely sure they got the message.

"I'm going to let you all know that I personally will recommend mutiny—and death will be the penalty."

Percy Robinson stood in shocked silence, thinking, "He can't be telling the truth."

A few of the men in the ranks began crying quietly.

"I've got a wife and kids," someone said.

"How could it be a mutiny?" Martin Bordenave wondered. "I didn't talk to nobody. I didn't conspire with nobody. I just made up my mind I was tired of it, you know. I wanted to be a sailor."

"Man, this guy can't have nobody shot," Jack Crittenden said to the man beside him. "They can't do this. Shoot somebody in the United States."

"He said it."

"Well, hell, he can't order someone to shoot you."

Each of the three lieutenants stepped up to his division.

"I have been ordered by my superior officers to order you men to go to work," Delucchi announced to Division Four. "All men that are willing to obey all orders anywhere at any time, fall in behind me."

The men faced a life-changing decision, with just seconds to make it.

Joe Small felt a moment of indecision as he watched the men separate into two groups. He took a step toward Lieutenant Delucchi—but stopped, and thought again.

"I concentrated on what he had said," Small later explained, "then I went back over to the other side. I realized the order could be to load ammunition, and that's one order I wasn't willing to obey."

In Percy Robinson's head, it was the admiral's last sentence that echoed loudest. "We didn't even know what mutiny meant," he later said. "We thought mutiny was something like when you kill people or take over something. We didn't know you could define disobeying orders as being mutiny. We thought mutiny could only happen on a ship."

But he had no doubt about the seriousness of Admiral Wright's threat. "And so I'm not going to give them a chance to shoot me," Robinson decided. "I'll go back to work."

Of the 258 men on the baseball field, 214 lined up behind their lieutenants. Forty-four men stood apart.

In the unwilling group, Willie Gay tried to cut the tension with a bit of bitter humor. "You gonna let them shoot you blindfolded?" he asked Jack Crittenden. "Or you gonna be looking at them?"

THE FIFTY

JOE SMALL AND THE OTHER forty-three were marched back to the pier. They spent another night on the prison barge.

The next morning, guards led six more sailors onto the barge—these six had initially agreed to return to work, but had wavered when it came time to load. All fifty prisoners were then taken by bus to Camp Shoemaker and locked in the brig. Only Small was placed in solitary confinement.

Four days later, a marine guard unlocked the door to Small's cell and said, "The admiral wants to talk to you."

Small was led to a private room. The guard shut the door, leaving Joe Small alone in the office with Admiral Carleton Wright.

"Small, you are the leader of this bunch," Wright said. "If you return to work, the rest of the men will."

Small said he would not return to the same work under the same conditions.

Wright glared at him. "If you don't return to work, I'm going to have you shot."

"You bald-headed son of a so-and-so, go ahead and shoot!"

That's how Small later described it—in fact, he used a word a lot harsher than *so-and-so*. It couldn't have helped his case.

As he was led back to prison, Small cooled off. He wished he hadn't lost his temper. "That branded me as a mutineer," he thought.

What he didn't regret was his refusal to give in.

"What they expected me to do was to just go back to duty and forget everything. They assumed that if I went back to duty everybody would follow me. But I had what I considered a legitimate reason for not going back to work."

Robert Routh, the Port Chicago sailor who'd been blinded in the blast, followed the story from his hospital bed.

"Go on brothers," he said to himself when his doctor updated him on the refusal of the fifty prisoners. If not for the wounds in his eyes, Routh knew, it would be fifty-one.

Back at the brig, Small was locked up with the other prisoners.

"Small, how do you feel about going back to work?" one of the men asked him.

"I'm not going," Small said.

"What if they shoot you?"

"Well, let 'em shoot. Because I'd sooner die by a bullet than an explosion."

Privately, though, Small was just as shocked by the charge as any of the men.

"I, for one, didn't consider refusing to work mutiny," he explained later. "We didn't try to take over anything. We didn't try to take command of the base. We didn't try to replace any officers; we didn't try to assume an officer's position. How could they call it mutiny?"

From a legal standpoint, Small's understanding of mutiny was pretty accurate. The Navy defined mutiny as "an unlawful opposition or resistance to or defiance of superior military authority, with a deliberate purpose to usurp, subvert, or override such authority."

Had Small and the others really tried to seize authority from the officers? He clearly thought they had not.

In his official report on the case to Admiral Wright, Captain Nelson Goss said he was not surprised by the behavior of the men from Port Chicago. "There are undoubtedly agitators, ringleaders, among these men," Goss wrote. "They have always been present since such personnel were first received at this depot."

From the very beginning, the captain explained, he'd tried his best to work with the black sailors. "Particular care," he wrote, "combined with patience, was exercised in outlining to these men the needs of the situation which required their services."

But no matter how patient he was, claimed Goss, the sailors displayed "a consistent attitude towards discrimination; never justified, as far as I could ascertain." He added: "The disposition, however, to seek opportunity to complain against fancied discrimination has always been present among present-day Negro enlisted personnel."

Admiral Wright sent his own report to the new Secretary of the Navy, James Forrestal, who'd taken over the job in May. After outlining the facts, Wright added his personal theory of the cause of the trouble. "The refusal to perform the required work arises from a mass fear arising out of the Port Chicago explosion. This fear is unreasonably associated with the handling of ammunition in ships."

That was it, just irrational fear. The way Wright saw it, neither the Navy's racial policies nor the chaotic working conditions on the pier played any part in the men's refusal to return to work.

"A considerable portion of the men involved are of a low order of mentality," the admiral commented, echoing a prejudice held by many officers. Wright defended the use of black sailors to load ammunition—and yet he admitted that it looked very bad to have only black sailors doing the loading. At the end of his report, Wright asked permission to make a major change. He wanted to begin training white sailors to work some of the shifts at Port Chicago and Mare Island.

Secretary of the Navy
James Forrestal

Secretary Forrestal approved the change and passed Wright's report to President Roosevelt. Roosevelt sent a brief note back to Forrestal, suggesting light punishments for the 208 men who had eventually agreed to go back to work. "They were activated by mass fear," commented Roosevelt. "This was understandable."

As for what to do with the fifty sailors still refusing to work, Roosevelt left that to the Navy. But he forwarded the report to his wife, Eleanor Roosevelt, writing "for your information" on the top. This was significant, because he knew Eleanor met often with black leaders, and was an outspoken critic of racial discrimination.

He knew she'd keep an eye on the case of the alleged mutineers.

In accordance with the president's suggestion, the Navy gave the men who had returned to work the relatively light punishment of losing three months' pay.

The fifty young men in the Camp Shoemaker brig—half of them teenagers—were officially charged with mutiny. The fifty, Admiral Wright's charge specified, had "conspired each with the other to mutiny against the lawful authority of their superior naval officers."

The job of leading the prosecution went to Lieutenant Commander James Coakley. An experienced prosecutor, Coakley had served as assistant district attorney of Alameda County, California, before the war.

Coakley spent the next few weeks gathering evidence against the accused, with a special focus on Joe Small.

"Small was supposed to be the ringleader," Edward

CONFIDENTIAL

MEMORANDUM FOR THE PRESIDENT:

1. Following the explosion at the Port Chicago Pier on the night of 17 July 1944 it became necessary to evacuate some of the enlisted personnel from the barracks at that activity and three divisions of negro enlisted personnel, consisting of 32_ men, were transferred to the Naval Ammunition Depot, Mare Island, California for duty.

2. On the afternoon of 10 August 1944 the three divisions of negro enlisted personnel refused to perform their assigned duty of handling ammunition to be discharged from a merchant vessel then berthed at Mare Island. When the orders to work were repeated to the men individually, 70 of them obeyed, but 255 continued to refuse to carry out the orders. The men were informed with great care of the needs of the situation, their obligation to obey orders and their opportunity to be of especial service.

3. On 12 August 1944 the Commandant of the Twelfth Naval District visited the Naval Ammunition Depot at Mare Island and addressed the insubordinate group of 255 men. The men were given an opportunity to explain the reason for their refusal to handle ammunition and thereafter were again required to state whether they would comply with orders. All but 44 of the men stated that they would do so. However, 6 others again changed their minds and refused to work at the assigned duty of unloading ammunition from a ship. 4 The Commandant reports that the refusal to perform the required work arises from a mass fear arising out of the Port Chicago explosion. This fear is unreasonably associated with the handling of ammunition in ships, rather than in the handling of ammunition as such.

5. The recalcitrant 44 and the 6 others who changed their minds were all transferred to the Naval Training and Distribution Center, Shoemaker, California to await further action.

6. As a result of the above incident the Commandant of the Twelfth Naval District reports that no action will be taken against the 70 men who first refused duty but who later obeyed when given orders individually. The 208 men who refused duty but later complied with orders after being addressed by the Commandant will be tried by summary courts martial on charges of refusing to obey orders. The 50 men who have continued to override authority will be brought to trial by general courts martial on charges of mutiny.

7. A copy of the complete report in this matter is attached hereto.

No white enlisted personnel are performing similar work at the naval ammunition depot or the naval magazine. To avoid any semblance of discrimination against negroes the Chief of the Bureau of Naval Personnel has authorized

Waldrop, one of the fifty, later explained. "What they wanted you to do, they wanted you to hang numbers on Small."

Coakley questioned many of the fifty personally. In his session with Waldrop, the lawyer demanded to know if Small had led the mutiny.

"No," Waldrop responded.

"Well, somebody has got to be the leader," Coakley insisted. "Everybody needs a leader."

"Nobody made me do nothing. We don't need a leader if you know what's going on on that base."

Jack Crittenden was questioned by James Tobin, the lieutenant of his division, with a marine guard looking on.

"Jack, I'm here to help you," Tobin began. "You're in trouble, and I'm here to help you."

"Yeah, it looks like I'm in trouble—I got a big *P* on me," Crittenden said, tapping the *P* for prisoner sewn to his shirt.

"Tell me what happened on the barge," Tobin demanded.

"Lieutenant, I don't know what went on on that barge. I was a scared jackrabbit on the barge."

"Jack, you're not being very cooperative."

This became a common theme of the interrogations. The officers wanted details about the meeting on the barge, the one at which Small had spoken to the group. Coakley was convinced this gathering was a central part of Small's secret plan, and he wanted to know exactly what had been said.

"I didn't say the things he wanted to hear," Crittenden remembered. "That made the marine guard so mad I thought he was going to beat me up when I came out of there."

A memo from James Forrestal addressed to the president outlines the events at Mare Island and recommends charges for those involved.

Guards later led Joe Small into the office of Lieutenant Louis Bannon, a legal officer at Camp Shoemaker. James Coakley was there too.

As Coakley listened, Bannon asked Small how it was that the men of Division Four had just happened to come to a stop in the road on the morning of August 9.

"How was it that the men refused to march," asked Bannon, "or stopped marching when they were given the order 'Column left'?"

"I guess they sensed something wrong," Small said.

Bannon wasn't satisfied. The refusal to march *had* to have been planned ahead of time, he said. "With whom had you talked about whether or not you would go down and load ships?"

"No one."

"You had never talked to a soul about it?"

"No, sir."

"Did anyone talk to you about it?"

"The boys did, yes, sir," said Small. "Many of them."

"Who were some of the boys who talked to you?" demanded Bannon.

"Practically everybody in the division."

"Let's get some names."

"I couldn't give their names unless I gave the names of the whole division. There wasn't one that didn't have something to say on that subject."

"You were a leader selected by the men," Bannon said. "They had faith in you, and the officers accepted you as a leader of the men."

Small didn't deny it. And he freely admitted that before August 9, many of the men had talked in the barracks about what they would do when they were ordered back to work loading ammunition. But he insisted there had been no organized plan to stop in the road, and that he had never tried to convince anyone to refuse to load.

Bannon turned to the barge meeting of August 10. He wanted to see if Small would admit to having called the men together for a talk.

Small did, explaining his goal had been to try to prevent a deadly eruption of violence between prisoners and guards.

"Did anybody else talk at that meeting besides you?" Bannon asked.

"No one else spoke at the meeting except myself, no, sir."

Back in his cell, thinking over the questions he'd been asked, Small realized what a deep hole he was in. Clearly, the officers saw him as the leader of a carefully crafted rebellion. They believed Small, in midnight barracks meetings, had convinced the men of his division to join him in mutiny.

It simply hadn't been like that, Small knew.

"It wasn't discussed," he later explained. "The Navy in their action, in their handling of our lives, had brought us down to the point where this was the necessary course of action. And there was nothing to discuss."

But Coakley had his theory, and was determined to prove it in court.

One by one, he called in the men who had agreed to go back to work after Admiral Wright's speech. He knew these men were hoping for light punishments, and he expected they'd be more willing to talk than the accused mutineers. Some were.

Several confirmed that there had been talk in the barracks in the nights before August 9; discussions about whether to go back to handling ammunition. Others told Coakley about the barge meeting. At Coakley's urging, the men tried to recall the words Small had used on the barge. As is always the case with eyewitnesses, different people remembered the same scene differently. But a few told Coakley that Small had said something about sticking together and having the officers "by the balls." No, it was "by the ass," someone else reported. Another remembered "by the tail."

Whatever the exact phrase, Coakley was now absolutely convinced that Small had not spoken to the men to prevent violence, as he claimed. Small's true goal, Coakley believed, had been to keep the group unified—to stop anyone who was wavering from giving in and going back to work.

Coakley was sure the fifty men were guilty of premeditated mutiny. He was sure that Joe Small had planned and orchestrated the whole thing.

The court-martial of the Port Chicago fifty was set to open on September 14.

The Navy hastily assigned Lieutenant Gerald Veltmann, a thirty-four-year-old lawyer from Texas, to lead the defense. Veltmann was given four young lawyers to assist him. The process was so rushed, the lawyers didn't even have time to meet with each of the accused before the trial began.

"I figured we'd go to trial, and then get shot," recalled Martin Bordenave.

But Veltmann was hopeful. As he raced to prepare, the defense lawyer spotted what he thought were a few weaknesses in the case against the accused mutineers.

When asked later to describe his mood in the days leading up to the court-martial, Veltmann replied, "Oh I would say it was calm. I don't think anyone had their heads hanging down, or their tails between their legs. I wasn't, at that time, old enough to be afraid of anybody."

TREASURE ISLAND

ON THE MORNING of September 14, 1944, the fifty accused men put on their dark blue uniforms and lined up outside a wooden barracks on Treasure Island in San Francisco Bay. The views from the little island were spectacular: the skylines of San Francisco and Oakland, the Golden Gate Bridge, the blue bay busy with ships steaming in and out.

But the men were in no mood to appreciate a beautiful view. At about 10 a.m., marine guards ordered them to march into the barracks. The building had been cleared of beds and set up as a courtroom. The sailors sat down in rows of seats along the back wall. Steam pipes hung from low ceilings above their heads. The walls around them were draped with flags.

Sitting behind a curving table on one side of the crowded space were Rear Admiral Hugh Osterhaus and the six other members of the court, all high-ranking naval officers. There is no jury in a court-martial. It would be up to Admiral Osterhaus and the other officers to hear the evidence in the case—and to decide the fate of the accused.

Opposite the judges were smaller tables; one for Lieutenant Commander Coakley and his team, and one for Lieutenant
Veltmann and his assistants. A few additional chairs had been
crammed into the barracks for newspaper reporters. Members
of the press were not normally invited to watch military trials, but this was no ordinary court-martial. This was the
largest mass trial in the history of the United States Navy,
and naval leaders did not want it shrouded in secrecy. Also,
they hoped the public trial would serve as a stark warning to
any other servicemen who may be thinking of bucking the
system.

When everyone was in place, James Coakley called on each
of the fifty accused in alphabetical order, asking every man the
same question: "You have heard the charge and specification
preferred against you; how plead you in the specification of the
charge, guilty or not guilty?"

All fifty responded the exact same way: "Not guilty, sir."

Coakley's strategy for the trial was to methodically build the
argument that there had been a conspiracy among the accused
sailors—that they had planned to refuse to work, and planned
to stick together no matter what. Step one was to lay out the
basics of what had happened at Mare Island.

He opened the prosecution by calling Commander Joseph
Tobin, Mare Island's executive officer. He asked Tobin to give a
summary of the events of August 9, the day the accused men
refused to work.

Tobin explained how he'd issued orders for the three divisions from Port Chicago to load the USS *Sangay*. He described

talking to many of the men individually after they'd stopped in the road.

"A number of the men took the attitude that they would obey any order, except to handle ammunition," said Tobin. "To those, I explained as clearly as I could, in brief, concise wording, that the choice of duty did not rest with any individual in the naval service."

Court-martial proceedings at Treasure Island, September 1944. Lieutenant Veltmann (center of photo) is seated with his team of lawyers.

Tobin then described how those still refusing to load were taken to the barge; how they were assembled several days later for Admiral Wright's talk; and how, even after being told they'd be charged with mutiny, these fifty accused still would not load ammunition.

Gerald Veltmann stood to cross-examine Commander Tobin. Veltmann had never defended accused mutineers before, but he understood Coakley's strategy. His plan was to undermine the prosecutor's case every step of the way. Right out of the gate, Veltmann sent a clear message that he was not intimidated—he was going to aggressively challenge Coakley's witnesses, even the high-ranking officers.

"Commander," Veltmann began, "I believe you stated that they said they [the accused men] would obey any order except loading ammunition, is that correct?"

"The attitude of the men was that they would obey what they chose to obey," Tobin replied.

"That wasn't the statement a while ago, was it, Commander?"

"That is the statement of fact regardless of what was stated earlier."

"Did they tell you they would obey any order they wanted to?" asked Veltmann.

"They implied that in the words they used."

"Did any of these men tell you, of the ones you talked to, did any of these tell you that they were willing to obey any order except loading ammunition?"

"A number did."

"In other words," Veltmann concluded, "there wasn't a complete disrespect of your authority?"

Coakley jumped to his feet. "Just a minute," he called to the judges. "That is objected to on the grounds it is too broad and indefinite and calls for the conclusion of this witness."

"I will withdraw the question," Veltmann said.

But he wasn't done with this line of questioning—in fact, it was vital to his strategy. According to the Navy's definition of mutiny, there had to be "a deliberate purpose to usurp, subvert or override" authority. The Port Chicago men may have resisted a specific order, but had they really tried to seize power from their superior officers? If not, they were not guilty of mutiny. Making this distinction clear, Veltmann believed, was his best chance to save the defendants' lives.

Moving on to the days following August 9, he continued to focus on the behavior of the fifty men.

"Did you ever have any riots?" Veltmann asked Tobin.

"No, we never had a riot."

"Did you ever have any trouble, specific riotous trouble with these fifty accused during the time, the ninth, tenth, or the eleventh of August?"

"Yes, we had trouble."

"With these fifty?"

"Yes."

"What was the trouble?"

"Refusing to obey orders."

"I am talking about their personal actions," Veltmann clarified. "I mean in connection with riotous actions?"

"There was."

"Did they storm about the depot? Just answer the question."

"Oh, no," said Tobin.

"Did they attack anybody?"

"No."

"Did they back you up in your office and tell you you couldn't order anybody to do anything?"

"No."

"Did they interfere with the prerogatives of your office in any way?"

Again Coakley jumped up to object.

"I am going to sustain that objection," Admiral Osterhaus told Veltmann. "The question you asked is certainly immaterial."

"I don't know that it is immaterial," Veltmann argued. "It is an element of mutiny, if it please the court, to usurp the power and authority of the commanding officer."

"The objection is sustained," Osterhaus ruled.

But Veltmann had made his point.

For his second witness, Coakley called the man he expected to give the most damaging testimony against the accused, Lieutenant Ernest Delucchi.

"If you recognize any of the accused, state whom," began Coakley.

The lieutenant stepped toward the prisoners. "Banks, stand up," he said. "Ernest Brown, third row, stand up." Delucchi identified Joe Small, Cyril Sheppard—a total of twenty-five men of the fifty were from his division.

Coakley asked Delucchi to describe the events of the morning of August 9.

"I passed the word myself over the loudspeaker for my division, the Fourth, to turn out for work," Delucchi explained. He described how Joe Small and the chief petty officer, Elmer Boyer, had helped get the division into formation.

"Now, while you were in front of your division," began Coakley, "did you hear any remarks from any of the men, either in your own division or the Eighth Division, with reference to whether they would go to work or not?"

"Yes, sir."

"Will you state what the remarks were?"

"I heard at least three times the statement: 'Don't go to work for the white motherf—ers.'" (Delucchi used the whole word in court.)

"Did you hear any other remarks like that?"

" 'Don't turn to for work.' "

This was devastating testimony, Coakley knew. The comments seemed to show that the men were hostile toward their officers, and planning to defy authority that day.

And it happened again on August 11, Delucchi testified. Admiral Wright had addressed the men on the baseball field, and Delucchi was walking up to his men to once again order them back to work.

"As you approached the division," Coakley coaxed his witness, "state whether or not you heard any remarks in the ranks of the men from your division."

"Yes, sir, I did."

"What did you hear?"

"Let's all stick together."

Coakley asked if Delucchi had heard anything else.

"Yes," Delucchi responded. "The first remark I heard was, 'The motherf—ers won't do anything to us; they are scared of us; they won't even send us to sea.' "

"Did you hear any other remark?"

"Yes, sir."

"What was it?"

"Let's run over the motherf—ers."

This was some of the most important testimony of the trial— and there's no way to know if it was true.

Coakley couldn't find a single witness to corroborate the quotes. The only other people who could possibly have heard them would be the defendants and other black sailors. Maybe they chose to forget a detail they knew would hurt the accused.

Or maybe, as many of the Port Chicago men believed, Delucchi was flat-out lying on the stand.

Either way, Gerald Veltmann knew the mere suggestion that sailors had used foul and threatening language toward their officer was sure to make a strong impression on the judges—all officers themselves. In his cross-examination, Veltmann skillfully limited the damage by exposing a major flaw in Delucchi's version of events.

"Now, you have attributed in the record a number of statements of profanity, or words that aren't used in common society, to some men," Veltmann said to Delucchi. "Isn't that right?"

"That is right, sir."

"Will you look at the accused and identify the men that said that?"

"I can't sir, because I had my back to them."

"Then when any of those statements were made you didn't see who made the statements?" Veltmann asked.

"No, sir."

"You don't know who made the statements?"

"No, sir."

"And you don't know absolutely that it was any member of your division?"

"Yes, sir," Delucchi insisted, "I am reasonably sure it was the men in my division."

"You say, 'reasonably sure.' I am asking if you know absolutely for sure."

"Yes, sir, I do."

"How do you know that?"

"For the simple reason that my division was behind me," said Delucchi, "and the wording came from behind me."

"The wording coming from behind you, do you know that it was any of these accused?"

"No, sir," Delucchi admitted, "I can't testify as to whether it was any of these men."

That was the key point Veltmann was trying to make. Satisfied, he sat down.

PROSECUTION

THE MUTINY TRIAL on Treasure Island was a minor story in most newspapers, overshadowed by bigger articles on American forces battling in Western Europe and the Pacific. But to African Americans across the country, this was an important story that would have to be watched closely.

"We concede the fact that a superior officer's command is to be obeyed, but we know that prejudice exists in the Navy," Irma Lewis, an Oakland woman, told a newspaper reporter. "We mothers want to know why these loading crews are all Negroes."

Joseph James, president of the San Francisco branch of the NAACP, was also following the story. "The Negro people are well aware of the pattern of discrimination practiced by the Navy," James told papers, "and they are very much concerned about this trial." James alerted the New York City headquarters, letting lead lawyer Thurgood Marshall know that this was a case worth watching.

The secretary of the Navy, James Forrestal, was keeping an eye on the trial from his office in Washington, D.C. Forrestal took a particular interest in the case, because he'd been thinking about the Navy's segregation policy. From his point of view, segregation was causing unnecessary problems. Treating black sailors like second-class citizens damaged the morale of the men, leading to headaches like the ongoing trial on Treasure Island. Also, it was wasteful to build separate barracks and classrooms, and it was wasteful to restrict black sailors to shore duty when men were needed on ships.

Forrestal was well aware of the basic assumption used to justify keeping the races separated—that packed together aboard ships black and white sailors simply wouldn't get along. He suspected it was nonsense.

With the backing of President Roosevelt, Forrestal approached Admiral Ernest King, Chief of Naval Operations.

"Admiral, I'd like to make a change in our racial policies," Forrestal began. "The President wants it, and I want it. How do you feel?"

"I don't know if we can do it," King said, "but if you want to try, I'll back you up every step of the way."

That summer, Forrestal and King began an experiment. The Navy assigned black sailors to serve alongside mostly white crews on twenty-five large, noncombat ships. King told the ships' commanding officers to report back on the results.

In the crowded courtroom on Treasure Island, James Coakley continued his prosecution.

After getting the testimony of the white officers, Coakley turned to a second set of witnesses—black sailors who had refused to load ammunition on August 9, but who had agreed to go back to work after Admiral Wright's threatening talk on August 11.

These witnesses were key for Coakley. It was his intention to show that the fifty accused mutineers had conspired together, enacting a secret plot they'd agreed upon ahead of time. The accused men denied that any such plot existed, but Coakley was hoping to get a different answer from some of the men who'd gone back to work.

Calling a sailor named Edward Johnson to the stand, Coakley asked him to describe any talk he'd heard in the barracks on the night of August 8.

"Well," Johnson said, "the boys didn't want to load ammunition because they were afraid."

"What else was said?" asked Coakley.

"Well, that was all I can remember."

"State whether or not anything was said by the men with reference to sticking together."

"Yes, sir, there was."

"State what was said."

"Well, the fellows said that they didn't want to load ammunition because they were afraid of it and that it would be better for the rest of us to stick together, that was all."

"What else?"

"That's all."

"At this time I certainly claim surprise!" Coakley shouted. One reporter described the lawyer as visibly annoyed with his witness. Clearly, he'd questioned Johnson in private before the trial, and now he was having trouble getting the sailor to repeat the story the way he wanted it.

Trying again, Coakley asked, "State whether or not you heard some men in the Second Division say, "If we stick together, the Navy won't do anything to us, we are too large a group."

"Yes, sir," Johnson said.

In his cross-examination, Veltmann went right after this seemingly damaging testimony. "Who made the statement, 'If we stick together, the Navy won't do anything to us, we are too large a group'?" he asked Johnson.

"I can't remember," Johnson said.

Gesturing to the men in the back of the room, Veltmann asked, "Can you identify the man of this fifty who made such statement, Johnson?"

"No, sir."

"Did you hear any of these fifty men say that they would not load ammunition?"

"No, sir."

"Did you ever try to get anyone not to load ammunition?"

"No, sir."

"Did any of these fifty try to get you not to load ammunition?"

"No, sir."

Coakley called several witnesses to testify about the so-called list—the mysterious document that had circulated in the barracks in the days before August 9. The list, Coakley hoped, would help show the existence of a mutiny plot.

On the stand, a sailor named Joseph Gray described being handed the list by a man in his division.

"What was on the paper?" Coakley asked.

" 'We, the undersigned men, are willing to work, but refuse to load ammunition.' "

"And you signed that paper?"

"Yes, sir," said Gray.

"What did you do with it after you signed it?"

"Passed it on to the fellow in the next bunk."

"How many names were on that paper?"

"Sixty or more."

In his cross-examination, Veltmann acknowledged that the list existed, but tried to show that it was not necessarily evidence of a secret plot.

"What was on the heading of that list?" he asked Joseph Gray.

Gray repeated what he had told Coakley: " 'We, the undersigned men, are willing to work, but refuse to handle ammunition.' "

"Was the word *refuse* on there?" asked Veltmann.

"I am not sure, sir."

"You are not sure?"

"No, sir."

"Could it be 'don't want to handle ammunition'?"

"Yes, sir, it could have been."

This was a crucial distinction—there's a big difference between "we refuse to handle ammunition" and "we don't want to handle ammunition." With the word "refuse," the list could be seen as evidence the men were planning to defy orders as a group. Without it, the list could be seen simply as the men's way of requesting a change of duty.

Again, Veltmann had done a good job of casting doubt on Coakley's case.

Another major topic for Coakley was the man he considered the ringleader of the mutiny—Joe Small. He asked his witnesses to describe anything they remembered hearing Small say before August 9.

"Well, I remember that some of the guys said they weren't going to load ammunition," a sailor named Edward Stubblefield testified. "Some of the guys said they were afraid to go on the docks."

"Do you know Small?" Coakley asked. "One of the accused here, Joe Small?"

"Yes, I know him, not personally; I just know him when I see him."

"Before the Eighth Division was mustered to go to work on the ninth of August, I will ask you whether or not you heard Small say anything?"

"No, sir, before the division was mustered to go to work, I didn't hear Small say anything."

Coakley blew up again. "I am going to impeach this witness right now!" he yelled. "This is contradictory, and it is detrimental to the case. I am very much surprised!"

Veltmann calmly objected that it would be ridiculous for Coakley to impeach Stubblefield—that is, to attack the credibility of his own witness. The judges agreed.

But the next day, Coakley called Stubblefield back to the stand. Again, Coakley asked him if Small had urged the men not to go to work. This time, the answer was different.

"Well, sir," the sailor said, "I heard Small say that the Fourth Division wasn't going to work, that it was up to the Eighth."

"When Small made the statement which you have just made, who was there?"

"There were several men of each division there."

Veltmann stood and asked the witness, "You testified yesterday, Stubblefield, didn't you?"

"Yes, sir."

"Didn't you say yesterday that you had heard Small say nothing?"

"No, sir."

"You are sure you didn't?"

"Yes, sir."

Stubblefield was obviously confused, or frightened, or simply lying. Anyway, he had completely changed his story and was now saying what Coakley wanted to hear.

Veltmann had no way of knowing which version the judges believed.

Coakley couldn't find any witnesses to corroborate the claim that Small had urged his fellow sailors not to work before August 9. But many witnesses *did* describe the meeting held on the barge on August 10, at which Small had definitely spoken to the group.

"What, if anything, did Small say?" Coakley asked Edward Stubblefield.

"He said the boys was in enough trouble, to obey the shore patrols and the officers, and he said if we all stick together, said they couldn't do anything with us and we had better obey the officers and the shore patrols because we was in enough trouble as it was, and we had the officers 'by the ass.' "

"And who was there when he said it?"

"Well, the whole group of men."

To Coakley, this was more evidence of Small's leadership role in the mutiny. Small called the meeting, Coakley insisted, to remind the men of their plot and to urge them to see it through.

Veltmann tried to show the court that Small's motives could be seen another way.

"At that meeting," he asked Stubblefield, "Small said the men should obey the shore patrol, that you were in enough trouble already?"

"Yes, sir."

"In other words, Small told you to stay out of trouble, didn't he?"

"Yes, sir."

"Didn't Small tell you to stick together in obeying the shore patrol?"

"He told us all to obey the shore patrol."

"And the purpose of that meeting was for discipline, wasn't it?" Veltmann asked.

"I will object to that," Coakley cut in, "on the grounds that it is calling for the conclusion of the witness."

"I will withdraw the question," Veltmann said.

But again, he'd made his point.

Coakley covered the same ground over and over again with his witnesses: there was talk in the barracks about not loading ammunition, there was a list of people who would not load, and Joe Small had called a meeting on the barge and spoken to the men.

With witness after witness, Veltmann showed that the talk in the barracks was vague, that it wasn't clear what the list had said, and that Small had spoken on the barge mainly to prevent violence.

"Did anybody ever try to convince you not to go to work?" Veltmann asked one sailor in a typical cross-examination.

"No, sir," the sailor said.

"Why didn't you go back to work?"

"Scared of ammunition."

"You made up your own mind not to go to work, is that it?"

"That's right."

This testimony was repeated with minor variations day after day. Several of the officers at the judges' table were seen nodding off at various points. One consistently snoozed after lunch.

Meanwhile, as the trial continued, family members of the accused mutineers worked to draw attention to the case. Several contacted the NAACP, urging the civil rights organization to provide legal help for the fifty.

Thurgood Marshall had heard enough; he was ready to take on the fight.

"There is no sufficient evidence of mutiny or conspiracy," Marshall told reporters in late September. "These men are being tried for mutiny solely because of their race."

Marshall asked for, and received, Navy Secretary Forrestal's permission to sit in on the trial. In early October, he got on a plane and flew to California.

JOE SMALL

COAKLEY WRAPPED UP his prosecution on day ten of the trial. The next day, Veltmann began calling witnesses for the defense.

Given that the fifty accused were facing a possible death sentence, Veltmann wanted to give every man a chance to speak in his own defense. It would take weeks, though, and the lawyer worried about losing the judges' attention. So he started with the defendants he considered most important.

Since Coakley was singling out Joe Small as the ringleader, Veltmann believed Small's explanation of his actions could swing the verdict one way or the other. He called Small to the stand and began by asking him to describe the events leading up to the so-called mutiny, starting with the explosion at Port Chicago.

"I was thrown out of my bed and got a few cuts around," Small said. "All the men were running wild here and there." The lights went out and the building began collapsing on them. "I got myself together and turned to help the other men out, the men that were injured."

Veltmann asked about the men's mood in the days after the blast.

They were tense and scared, Small explained. He started telling the story of the sailor who thought it was funny to jam his bedsheet into the fan and watch the other men panic.

"Just a minute," Coakley interrupted. "Objected to on the grounds it is immaterial. This is two or three weeks before the 9th of August."

"Objection overruled," said Admiral Osterhaus.

Small finished the story.

"Did anything else happen?" asked Veltmann.

"Yes, sir," said Small. "Another night similar to that, one of the boys dragged a bunk across the floor and same thing happened. The men started running, and he stopped dragging the bunk across the floor. There was cursing and swearing. I quieted them down and got them back to bed."

"Why did they run, Small?"

"Just a minute," Coakley cut in. "Objected to as calling for his conclusion."

"Objection sustained."

"Why did *you* run, Small?" Veltmann asked.

"Objected to as irrelevant and immaterial," called Coakley.

"Objection overruled."

"I did break to run at first," Small explained, "but I realized what it was, and I stopped."

"Why did you run the first time?"

"Because the first thing I thought of was an explosion."

"Did any of the men tell you why they ran?"

"Yes."

"Why?"

"Because they thought it was an explosion."

"From your observation, would you say that the men were afraid at that time?"

"Yes, sir."

This was an important point for the defense, which explains why Coakley worked so hard to prevent Small from making it. Veltmann wanted the judges to understand how terrified the young sailors were in the days after the Port Chicago blast. He wanted the court to consider the possibility that fear—not a secret plot—was really behind their refusal to load ammunition.

Veltmann then directly attacked Coakley's claim that there was a secret plot.

"Small, while you were at Shoemaker following the explosion at Port Chicago, did you attend any meetings with reference to refusing to load ammunition?"

"No, sir."

"Did you try to convince anyone not to load ammunition?"

"No, sir."

"Did anyone try to convince you not to load ammunition?"

"No, sir."

Veltmann asked Small about the list that circulated in the barracks. Small said, truthfully, that he hadn't signed it. He didn't mention he'd destroyed it.

Next, Veltmann asked about the now-famous barge meeting. Earlier in the trial, Lieutenant Delucchi had testified that he had called Small aside before the men got on the barge. According to Delucchi, he simply asked Small to see that the men got on and off the barge in an orderly fashion.

Small's version of the conversation was different.

"Now, when you were put on the barge," Veltmann asked, "did Lieutenant Delucchi say anything to you?"

"Yes, sir."

"What did he say?"

"I was to see to it that no rough stuff was carried on," Small said of his orders from Delucchi. "He told me, 'I am putting you in charge of the division, and I am giving you three men to work under you, and out of you four, you ought to be able to keep things straight.' "

It was with these orders in mind, Small explained, that he called the meeting on the barge. He saw trouble coming between the sailors and the guards, and he considered it his job to help defuse the situation.

"I stepped out where I thought that everyone could see me," Small described. "Then I went on to tell them that they had to knock off the horseplay, obey the S.P.s, the shore patrol, take orders that were given to them by the officers. . . . I told them also if they pulled together, they would find out that things would be much easier for them."

"What did you mean by that, Small?" asked Veltmann.

"I meant to pull together in keeping themselves straight, one to the other; if one got off wrong, it was up to his shipmate, his pal, whoever it might be, to tell him to 'straighten up and fly right,' knock it off, get back in line."

"In other words, you meant keep order, isn't that what you meant?"

"Yes, sir."

"Did you make the statement attributed to you by other witnesses that 'We have the officers by the ass'?"

"No, sir."

"Or 'We have the officers by the tail'?"

"No, sir."

"Or 'We have the officers by the balls'?"

"No, sir."

This seems to be the one case in which Small was untruthful on the stand. He later explained that Veltmann had privately advised him to deny having told the men "We have the officers by the balls." Small had wanted to explain to the court that he hadn't meant it as a threat, but was using language he knew would get the men's attention. But Veltmann didn't think the judges would accept this explanation.

Coakley stood up, eager to cross-examine the witness.

"How old are you, Small?" Coakley began.

"Twenty-three, sir."

Coakley knew this, of course, but wanted to remind the court that Small was older than most of the other defendants. The prosecutor was building his case on the theory that Small was their secret leader.

"You refused to march to the ship on the 9th of August, didn't you?" Coakley asked.

"Well, I stopped after I bumped into one of the petty officers that was walking ahead of me."

"I will ask you the question again; you refused to march to the ship on the 9th of August, didn't you?"

"We were never told we were going to the ship," Small replied. "We got the command 'Column left' and everyone stopped; I bumped into the petty officer, and I stopped too."

Coakley tried to show that Small knew exactly what the "Column left" order meant. Small didn't deny it.

"When you heard 'Column left' did you know what you were going to do?" asked Coakley.

"We had an idea."

"What was your idea?"

"That we were going to the ship."

"To load ammunition?"

"Yes, sir."

"Because when you got 'Column left' that would take you down to the river where the ferry was to take you across to the ship; is that right?"

"Yes, sir."

"And you had made up your mind before that that you were not going to handle ammunition, hadn't you?"

"Yes, sir."

Coakley paused. He apparently hadn't expected Small to concede this point—and wanted to make sure the judges didn't miss it. "You had made up your mind that you would obey any orders except the order to handle ammunition?"

"Yes, sir."

Coakley was getting so excited he started repeating himself.

"When the division got a 'Column left' order, you realized you were going to the ship, didn't you?"

"Object to the question as having been asked and answered," Veltmann pointed out.

"Withdraw the question," Coakley said.

But he couldn't help himself. "At that time when the division, the Fourth Division, received the command 'Column left,' you refused to go, didn't you?"

"I had to stop," Small said. "I bumped into the petty officer; I couldn't walk over on top of him."

"Will you answer that question yes or no?" Coakley demanded. "Either you refused to go or you didn't."

"I didn't go."

"You refused to go, didn't you?"

Veltmann objected again. "He has already answered the question."

"Withdraw the question," said Coakley.

At this point Admiral Osterhaus declared it was time to break for lunch.

An hour and twenty minutes later, Small was back on the stand, and the cross-examination continued. Coakley tried again and again to get Small to admit that he had convinced his fellow sailors not to load ammunition. Small refused to budge from the exact same story he'd been telling all along. Yes, before August 9 there had been a lot of talk among the men about how they might react if ordered to load ammunition. And yes, Small had made up his mind not to load. But no, he had not tried to influence anyone else, and there had been no secret plot.

Frustrated, Coakley moved on to another key point, the barge meeting.

"Now then, you called the meeting, didn't you?"

Small explained that he had talked with a few other men on the barge, and they agreed, together, to hold a meeting.

"Answer the question yes or no, either you did or you didn't."

"I had a part in calling it."

Veltmann jumped back up to clarify a crucial detail about the barge meeting.

"Why did you call the meeting?" he asked Small.

"Well, because I felt that it would help in getting the boys to do right, discipline on the barge, different things that needed to be done."

"In other words, you were performing, then, the duty as a petty officer that Lieutenant Delucchi ordered you to do?"

"Yes, sir."

Coakley didn't accept this. "Did Lieutenant Delucchi tell you to hold a meeting on the barge?" he asked Small.

"No, sir."

"Then you weren't performing any duties as a petty officer when you called a meeting, were you?"

"He did not give me orders to call a meeting," explained Small, "but he told me to keep discipline on the barge, and I felt that that was the best way to speak to all the men at one time."

"You weren't even a petty officer?"

"No, sir."

"You never have been a petty officer?"

"No, sir."

These types of exchanges continued all afternoon.

Thurgood Marshall sat with the newspaper reporters, watching, listening, planning his next moves.

"Defense counsel are good and know what they are doing," he wrote of Veltmann and his team in a letter to NAACP head Walter White. "Prosecutor is vicious and dumb. There is no evidence of mutiny."

Between sessions in court, he visited with the prisoners.

"I'm Thurgood Marshall," he told the men. "I'm the chief special counsel for the NAACP. And we have taken an interest in this case, and we're watching this."

"He just said to play it cool, and he was working, he was working on it," Freddie Meeks remembered. "And he really did go to bat for us."

Although Marshall liked what he saw of Veltmann as a courtroom lawyer, he wasn't happy with the overall strategy of the defense. Nothing at all was being said about the Navy's unequal treatment of black sailors. Nothing was said of the segregation at Port Chicago, or the unsafe working conditions. Without looking honestly at these factors, the court would never get at the true cause of the men's refusal to load ammunition.

The fifty defendants felt exactly the same.

"The defense strategy, to me it was a mockery," Martin Bordenave later said.

"The guy who was defending us, he didn't have no defense," Edward Waldrop added.

Joe Small was equally irritated that the whole truth wasn't being heard. In private, he told the defense lawyers all about the problems at Port Chicago. "I discussed it with them lengthily," he later explained. "Working conditions, and the betting among the officers. But it didn't come out in the trial."

As frustrating as this was, Small was smart enough to figure out what was going on. The defense lawyers were all naval officers—they weren't going to bring out details that would be embarrassing to the Navy. And even if they'd wanted to, the judges wouldn't have let them.

"We couldn't volunteer any information, we could only answer questions that were put to us," Small explained. "And if you volunteered anything, they would tell you, 'Please answer the questions yes or no.' So you didn't get a chance to bring out any information that they didn't want brought out."

The whole trial gave Albert Williams the unsettling feeling of being a kid and being accused by an adult of something he hadn't done. "That was the atmosphere there," he said of the mood in the courtroom. "No matter what you say, you're going to get this whipping. Whether you're right or wrong, somebody did it—and you're going to get whipped."

THE VERDICT

VELTMANN SPENT the next two weeks calling each of the accused mutineers. By letting each man speak, he hoped to show the court that this was hardly a cohesive group of conspirators. Rather, this was a bunch of very young men, with different stories, and different reasons for doing what they did.

For instance, John Dunn, one of the defendants, weighed just 104 pounds. A Navy doctor had specifically told him he wasn't strong enough to load ammunition. Dunn was working as mess cook on the morning of August 9, but Lieutenant James Tobin ordered him down to the loading pier anyway.

"I told him the doctor told me I was too light to work on the dock," Dunn testified. "He said, 'That makes no difference.'"

Tobin told Dunn to step over with those who refused to work, and Dunn was marched to the prison barge.

Another defendant, Julius Dixson, had suffered dizzy spells on the pier. Lieutenant Delucchi considered the man a hazard to his entire division and agreed when a doctor declared him unfit for loading. Dixson spent the day of August 9 working in the mess hall and didn't even know about the Division Four men getting the "Column left" order and stopping in the road. But on Delucchi's orders, a lieutenant named Eugene Kaufmann confronted Dixson in the kitchen.

"Dixson, you can't be a mess cook forever," Kaufmann chided.

"I am not able to load ammunition," Dixson replied.

Hearing that, Kaufmann ordered Dixson to report to the barge and join the other prisoners. Both Dixson and Dunn were counted among the fifty accused mutineers—without ever having been ordered to load.

Ollie Green was another sailor with a unique story. Wounded in the face and chest by flying glass in the Port Chicago blast, Green was back on duty with Division Four in early August. But then, on August 8, he fell while running to chow, fracturing his left wrist.

Green told the court that on the morning of August 9, he'd been lying in bed when the division mustered for work. He lay around a while longer, and then left the barracks with his arm in a sling. By the time he strolled outside, the men had already stopped in the road, and Chaplain Flowers was out there trying to persuade them to go to work.

"Are you willing to go back to work loading ammunition?" Flowers asked Green.

"No, sir," Green said, explaining that his wrist was killing him, and the doctor had put him on the sick list.

Green wanted to talk with Lieutenant Delucchi, but never got the chance—he was sent right to the prison barge. He testified that he was afraid of ammunition, but would have gone to load if he'd been specifically ordered to do so. He never was.

"What, then, was the reason that you said no?" Coakley asked in his cross-examination. "Because you had a broken wrist or because you were afraid of ammunition, which was it?"

"I had a broken wrist *and* I was afraid of ammunition," said Green.

"Both of them?"

"Yes, sir."

"If you hadn't had a broken wrist, would you have said yes?"

"Yes, sir."

After Coakley's questions, Admiral Osterhaus asked Green the same exact question he asked every witness at the end of his testimony: "Do you have anything further to state?"

This was a mere formality—witnesses were expected to say, "No, sir," and return to their seats. Ollie Green shocked everyone in the room by going off script.

"I got a couple of things to say, sir," Green told the admiral.

Both Veltmann and Coakley looked on in shocked silence as the witness continued.

"The reason I was afraid to go down and load ammunition, them officers, the guys down there loading ammunition, racing each division to see who put on the most tonnage, and I knowed the way they was handling ammunition, it was liable to go off again."

Green looked out at the room of stunned faces, and added, "This is my reason for not going down there."

Newspapers rushed to print the story of Green's unexpected testimony. The Navy responded with a statement denying the charge—there had been no racing and no betting at Port Chicago.

One by one, Veltmann called the accused men to the stand. Though each sailor's memory of events was slightly different, a few main points were repeated over and over.

Nearly every man testified that he was afraid of ammunition after the Port Chicago blast. Not a single one attended secret meetings, or joined a plan not to load. Most had seen lists requesting a change of duty circulating in the barracks in the days before August 9. Some had signed, some hadn't. And just about everyone recalled Joe Small speaking to the group on the barge on August 10. The gist of Small's talk was that he was trying to keep order.

In his cross-examinations, Coakley tried again and again to get at least one defendant to admit to being a part of a mutiny plot. No luck. He tried again and again to get someone to say that Joe Small was behind the whole thing. No one did.

The prosecutor's rising frustration became obvious as he questioned a sailor named Frank Henry. Henry testified he had signed a list that stated "The below signed men are afraid to handle ammunition and would like some change of duty."

Coakley simply could not accept this. He wanted to know what else was on the paper, how tall the paper was, how wide, how many names were on it.

"I couldn't say," Henry said about the number of names.

"Was it full or half-full?" demanded Coakley.

"It was just about three-quarters full."

"Was it signed in one column or in two columns?"

"It was one column when I signed it."

"When was that?"

"I couldn't say."

"How long before the ninth of August?"

"I couldn't say."

Coakley finally burst, shouting, "Where did you take your boot training?"

"Great Lakes."

"Did you learn to say 'sir' when you talk to an officer? Did you learn that?"

"Yes, sir."

"Why don't you say it instead of being so insolent?"

Veltmann objected to this hostile attack.

"He hasn't said it either to you or to me as yet," Coakley complained to Veltmann.

"He has said, 'Yes, sir,' a number of times," Veltmann pointed out.

Admiral Osterhaus sustained the objection.

The testimony of Alphonso McPherson, one of the fifty, ignited Coakley's biggest tantrum. McPherson described being interrogated by Coakley a few days after August 9. Coakley had seemed unhappy with McPherson's answers and finally said, "I'll give you one more chance. Come clean or I'll see that you get shot."

Hearing this, Coakley leaped to his feet, flushing red and shouting, "You are sure of that?"

"Yes, sir," McPherson insisted, "I am sure you told it to me."

Coakley tried to shake McPherson from his story but couldn't. He turned to Admiral Osterhaus.

"This thing was injected into the record which I claim is not true, I never told him he was going to be shot," Coakley moaned. "I am not trying to conceal anything here, and I am very indignant about it. It is hitting below the belt, that's all it is, if it please the court."

The entire courtroom exploded into laughter—defendants, lawyers, reporters, even the judges. The admiral had to slam his gavel on the table to restore order.

Coakley's aggressive outbursts convinced Thurgood Marshall that something was very wrong in the Treasure Island courtroom.

During tense trials, Marshall was fond of urging his staff to keep cool. "Lose your head, lose your case," was his motto. But after a week on Treasure Island, Marshall was having trouble following his own rule.

"The NAACP is going to make it its job to expose the whole rotten Navy setup which led to the Port Chicago explosion, and in turn to the so-called 'mutiny' trial of fifty Negro sailors now taking place," Marshall announced at a meeting of the NAACP in San Francisco. "This is not an individual case. This is not fifty men on trial for mutiny. This is the Navy on trial for its whole vicious policy toward Negroes.

"Negroes are not afraid of anything any more than anyone else," he said. "Negroes in the Navy don't mind loading ammunition. They just want to know why they were the only ones doing the loading! They want to know why they are segregated, why they don't get promoted!"

As for James Coakley, Marshall told the crowd, the man obviously had a problem with black sailors, and his prejudice was making it impossible for the defendants to get a fair trial.

Two days later, Marshall issued a statement calling on the Navy to open an investigation into the Port Chicago disaster and trial. The defense lawyers were doing a good job, Marshall said, but the court-martial wasn't even scratching the surface of the real issues behind the so-called mutiny.

"A Navy Department investigation would clear up a lot of questions which are in my mind about this whole situation," Marshall told the press. "For instance, I want to know why, at the time of the explosion at Port Chicago, every man loading ammunition there was a Negro."

He challenged the Navy to explain its policy of segregation and to explain why black sailors were put to work on the loading docks with no training. "I want to know why commissioned officers at Port Chicago were allowed to race their men. I want to know why bets ranging from five dollars up were made between division officers as to whose crew would load more ammunition."

While Marshall waited for answers, the lawyers on Treasure Island made their closing arguments.

Coakley spent four hours hammering away at the points he'd been making for the past six weeks. After the Port Chicago explosion, he charged, the men knew they'd be ordered to load ammunition again soon—and secretly began plotting to resist. As evidence, Coakley reminded the court of the lists that many of the defendants had signed. He reminded judges of Delucchi's testimony about hearing offensive remarks from the men. "Don't go to work for the white motherf—ers," Coakley quoted. "And he heard that three times."

After the men refused to load ammunition, Coakley continued, they were packed onto the prison barge, where many of the sailors had second thoughts about defying their officers. But rather than letting anyone break with the group, Joe Small called a meeting.

"Now, that was a mutinous assembly," Coakley told the judges, "that was a mutinous meeting. After it ended, there was cheering and clapping."

"These fifty men are guilty," concluded Coakley. "There is ample evidence to sustain a conviction of all of these fifty men."

The next morning, day thirty-three of the trial, Gerald Veltmann took his turn.

"Gentlemen, we speak now for the accused," he began, "for these fifty men who are here charged with mutiny."

Veltmann read the Navy's definition of mutiny: "An unlawful opposition or resistance to or defiance of superior military authority, with a deliberate purpose to usurp, subvert, or override such authority." Then he asked the judges, "In what way have these accused gentlemen, usurped, subverted, or overridden their superior military authority?"

All the evidence offered by the prosecution, Veltmann insisted, broke down upon closer examination. Take the list that some men signed in the barracks. "What was the list for?" asked Veltmann. "It was a list of men who didn't want to handle ammunition, and can you wonder at that?"

Was there really "mutinous talk" in the barracks in the days leading up to August 9? "The record shows no such talk," said Veltmann. Men talked of the Port Chicago explosion, sure, and of their fear of ammunition. "And what would be more natural than the discussion and exchange of views by the men that underwent that experience? This is not conspiracy; that is not scheming; that does not provide the essential elements of mutiny."

What about the obscene remarks supposedly overheard by

Lieutenant Delucchi on August 9? No one else heard them, Veltmann reminded the court. Besides, even Delucchi couldn't say with any certainty that the remarks were made by one of the fifty defendants.

Was Joe Small really a devious ringleader? Look at that incident at Camp Shoemaker, when that joker stuck a sheet into the fan and the men panicked. "Who calmed them and restored order?" asked Veltmann. "Yes, Joe Small, a member of the Fourth Division, whom Lieutenant Delucchi chose to keep order elsewhere, on the barge."

Sure, Small spoke at that barge meeting and urged the men to "stick together"—stick together in obeying orders and maintaining discipline.

Veltmann reminded the court of the stories of Dunn and Dixson, the men taken off loading duty by doctors, and of Oliver Green, the sailor with the broken wrist. How could these men be considered mutineers?

The bottom line, Veltmann insisted, was that the prosecution had presented no reliable evidence of any kind of plot, or any attempt to seize authority from officers. "And without proof of these elements," Veltmann concluded, "the case of the prosecution most certainly has not been proven."

"Gentlemen, that completes our argument, and we submit that these fifty men are not guilty of the offense of mutiny."

The court was cleared at 11:55 a.m. After an eighty-minute lunch break, everyone returned and Admiral Osterhaus announced the verdict.

All fifty men were found guilty of mutiny.

The judge advocate was recalled and directed to record the sentence of the court as follows:

The court, therefore, sentences him, Joseph R. Small, seaman first class, U.S. Naval Reserve, to be reduced to the rating of apprentice seaman, to be confined for a period of fifteen (15) years, then to be dishonorably discharged from the United States naval service, and to suffer all the other accessories of said sentence as prescribed by section 622, Naval Courts and Boards.

Hugo W. Osterhaus,
Rear Admiral, U. S. Navy, Retired, President.

Edward S. Jackson,
Captain, U. S. Navy, Retired, Member.

Lloyd S. Shapley,
Captain, U. S. Navy, Retired, Member.

Cornelius W. Flynn,
Captain, U. S. Navy, Member.

Alexander B. Hayward,
Commander, Medical Corps, U. S. Navy, Retired, Member.

Thomas E. Flaherty,
Commander, U. S. Navy, Retired, Member.

Gregory P. Maushart,
Lieutenant, U. S. Naval Reserve, Member.

James F. Coakley,
Lieutenant Commander, U. S. Naval Reserve,
Judge Advocate.

HARD LABOR

CYRIL SHEPPARD FELT a rush of terror when he heard the verdict.

"My knees almost hit the ground," he remembered. His first thought was of his newborn daughter at home—would he ever see her?

"The verdict was guilty," Joe Small recalled, "guilty as charged." Small was shaken by the news, but not exactly surprised. "I expected it, from the way that the trial went."

Small and the others were led back to the brig, where they waited several days to find out if they were going to be shot.

Finally, they were called together to hear the sentences read. All fifty sentences were identical—fifteen years of hard labor in prison, and dishonorable discharge from the Navy.

"Fifteen years," Jack Crittenden remembered thinking. "Here I ain't but nineteen years old." He quickly calculated how old he'd be when he got out. He wondered if his mother and father would still be alive.

Many of the men cried; many were too dazed to react.

"I tried to calm the men down," Small later said. He

All fifty sailors received handwritten sentences dictating identical terms.

assured the men they'd survive this; they'd be free again one day. "All you gotta do is keep your nose clean, and you'll get out."

The sentences were sent to Admiral Wright for his review. Wright knocked a few years off the jail terms of some of the youngest men. Small and nine others were ordered to serve the full fifteen.

In November, the Port Chicago fifty were handcuffed and taken to the Naval Disciplinary Barracks at Terminal Island in southern California, where the Navy confined serious offenders facing long sentences. The men were locked behind bars, two to a cell. In what seems like a cruel joke, each of the fifty was given a copy of the complete court-martial transcript—a foot-high pile of papers that only served to remind them of how bogus the trial had been.

"You can look all the way through there," Edward Waldrop said, "read all fifty men's statements, you will find no way in there that the government really proved that we mutinied."

"Everything was rigged," Small agreed.

Actually, Small may have been even closer to the truth than he knew. Decades after the trial, Gerald Veltmann revealed a shocking detail. Between courtroom sessions, while the accused men were still testifying, Veltmann had overheard Admiral Osterhaus say, "We're going to find them guilty."

The men had one hope—Thurgood Marshall was on the case.

Declaring the mutiny convictions "one of the worst frame-ups we have come across in a long time," Marshall promised to fight on. The Port Chicago fifty had been judged guilty of mutiny, but their real crime, he insisted—the thing that *really* got them in trouble—was drawing attention to the disgraceful way the United States Navy treated black sailors.

Marshall wrote directly to Secretary of the Navy James Forrestal, arguing that the Treasure Island trial had been completely unsatisfactory, leaving every key question unanswered.

"Why is it that the only naval personnel loading ammunition regularly were Negroes?" Marshall asked. "Why is it that these men were not given any training whatsoever in the dangers to be found in loading ammunition? Why is it that officers 'raced' their gangs in contests in the loading of ammunition?"

The people were demanding answers, Marshall insisted, and the answers needed to come from the top.

Forrestal must have cringed as he read this. He'd been hoping the whole embarrassing Port Chicago mess would blow over. Now, with Thurgood Marshall on the job, the story was not about to go away.

In his response, Forrestal assured Marshall that he'd looked over the case and had seen no convincing proof of unsafe conditions on the loading pier, or of officers betting on tonnage totals. He suggested that racism played no part in the Navy's treatment of the Port Chicago men. Why had only black sailors been assigned to load ammunition at Port Chicago? Simple, Forrestal explained: the base was manned almost entirely by black sailors. "Naturally, therefore, the only naval personnel loading ammunition regularly were Negroes."

Forrestal couldn't possibly have expected Marshall to buy such lame reasoning. But the secretary was not about to admit that the Navy deserved any of the blame for the Port Chicago explosion, or the so-called mutiny that followed.

Not in public, anyway.

Privately, Forrestal was more convinced than ever that

segregation was becoming a major aggravation for the Navy. And worse, an unnecessary one.

Captains were starting to report on the experiment begun that summer with integrated ship crews. After all of the Navy's hand-wringing about racial tensions on ships, white and black sailors shocked everyone by getting along fine.

"The assimilation of the general service Negro personnel aboard this ship has been remarkably successful," went one typical report from an integrated ship's commander. "To the present date there has been no report of any difficulty which could be laid to their color."

A similar report came in from one of President Roosevelt's sons, Franklin Roosevelt, Jr., who commanded a destroyer escort. He'd heard grumbling from some of the white crew when they first heard black sailors were coming aboard. Then the young men started living and working side by side. "Before we reached the Panama Canal my racial problem had vanished," Roosevelt reported.

Forrestal was encouraged, and he was determined to push integration further. Still, he had no intention of reducing the sentences of the Port Chicago mutineers.

In their cells on Terminal Island, the Port Chicago prisoners kept up with the story through letters from their families and articles in black newspapers. The NAACP helped spread the men's version of events by publishing a powerfully worded pamphlet on the case.

"The Navy has denied them every right of equality in the service," the pamphlet said of the imprisoned men. "It has denied them their rights as Americans to serve in active sea duty.

It has segregated them, insulted them, risked their lives by sheer unnecessary inefficiency, and now it will send them to a Federal penitentiary for years in order to save its own face."

Marshall sent the prisoners copies of the pamphlet. It was strong stuff, but the men had no idea if it would help. All they could do was try to adjust to the grinding daily routine, a mix of boredom and outdoor labor.

"Hard labor was anything they wanted you to do," Small recalled. Some days they wove ropes or made nets for ships. Some days they cleared driftwood from beaches or smashed big rocks into little rocks with sixteen-pound sledgehammers. Marines, armed with pistols and clubs, watched their every move.

Luckily for the Port Chicago sailors, they were respected—even feared—by both prisoners and guards. "We were celebrities," Small said. "We had a reputation for being unruly and bad."

Terminal Island could be a rough place, but the Port Chicago fifty were known as the guys who'd stood up to the U.S. Navy. Wherever they went, they heard men whispering, "There go the Port Chicago boys."

"Nobody bothered us," Small said.

Just as Forrestal feared, the Port Chicago story was not going away.

While Thurgood Marshall prepared an appeal on behalf of the convicted men, black newspapers printed editorials calling for justice. Thousands of people signed petitions demanding the Navy reopen the case. At the same time, more trouble at American military bases around the world only cranked up the pressure.

On the island of Guam in the South Pacific, rising tensions

between black sailors and white marines exploded on Christmas Eve, 1944. At a town near base, a group of marines were annoyed to see black sailors chatting with local women. The marines shot at the sailors, chasing them out of town. The next night, back on the base, the sailors jumped into trucks and headed toward the marine camp to fight it out. They were intercepted by military police and arrested. Forty-three black sailors were court-martialed, convicted of rioting, and thrown in jail.

At Camp Rousseau in California, black sailors faced all the same humiliations the Port Chicago men had—segregation, racist insults, the worst jobs, no promotions. Finally sick of it, they hit back with a hunger strike in early 1945. They'd follow orders, the sailors told their officers, and continue working, but they would not eat. The strike only lasted a couple of days, but the story got into the newspapers, focusing more attention on the military's unfair treatment of black servicemen.

Something had to be done, Forrestal decided.

Back when the war began, naval leaders had argued that racism was not their problem. The Navy had a war to win, and couldn't be expected to solve America's race problems at the same time. But things looked different after Port Chicago and these newer incidents. Segregation was actually *hampering* the war effort. It was time for a new plan—whether the country was ready for it or not.

The Navy assigned more black sailors to integrated crews aboard ships, and the first black naval officers were assigned to ships at sea. More white sailors were moved into unpopular shore duty assignments, like ammunition loading. The change was gradual. But it was real change.

"The Navy accepts no theories of racial differences in inborn ability," the Bureau of Naval Personnel informed all naval

Lester Granger during an inspection of facilities for black servicemen at Naval Air Station, San Diego, June 20, 1945.

officers in February 1945, "but expects that every man wearing its uniform be trained and used in accordance with his maximum individual capacity."

Forrestal appointed Lester Granger, an African American civil rights leader, as a civilian advisor. Granger's task: to tour bases all over the world, watch the integration process up close, and recommend ways to improve it. This was an absolutely stunning reversal from just four years before, when the Navy considered black men fit only to cook and clean.

But for fifty of the men who'd help force this change, there was no change. The Port Chicago fifty were still doing hard labor in southern California.

When they weren't outside working, the Port Chicago men hung out together, talking and playing cards. "We didn't socialize with the other prisoners too much," Edward Waldrop explained. "We stayed mostly to ourselves, by ourselves."

The men knew Thurgood Marshall was preparing their appeal. They knew any chance of winning would be blown if they got into trouble in prison. So they stuck close together, reminding each other of what Marshall had told them at Treasure Island. "Play it cool," he'd said. "I'm working."

In early April 1945, Marshall traveled to Washington, D.C. to present the appeal. Standing before a board of officers, he made his case.

"One day, sitting in at that trial, would convince you that there was something wrong," Marshall told the officers. The prosecution had painted the defendants as a unified group of plotters, but that just wasn't the reality. "They are all different," Marshall said of the fifty. "A couple of them are just plain kids."

Maybe they're guilty of resisting an order, Marshall suggested. That doesn't equal mutiny. Some of the most damning evidence of the entire trial came from the statements Lieutenant Delucchi reported overhearing: "Don't go to work for the white motherf—ers," and similar remarks. But Delucchi couldn't identify the men who said these things, and wasn't sure they even came from one of the accused.

Legally, this type of hearsay evidence should never have been allowed on the record—and James Coakley, a trained prosecutor, knew it. "He misled the court," Marshall charged. "He deliberately set upon a course of getting into the record evidence that he himself knows is inadmissible. When the evidence which is the meat of the so-called mutiny is inadmissible testimony, then the case has to fail."

As further proof the trial had been a sham, Marshall pointed out how little time the judges had spent reaching a verdict—an average of ninety-six seconds deciding each man's fate, assuming they didn't take time off for lunch. "In a case involving fifty men, you can't sit down in less than an hour, or a little over an hour, and give each one individual consideration as to which one is guilty and which one is not."

"I do not take up cases unless I am convinced that the men are innocent," Marshall told the board. "I was never so convinced that the evidence was insufficient in a case as I was in listening to that case."

"Justice can only be done," he concluded, "by a complete reversal of the findings."

The board members assured Marshall they would give full consideration to everything he had said. There was nothing more Marshall could do. He went back to New York and waited for news.

Behind the scenes, Navy lawyers studied the Treasure Island transcript—and agreed with Marshall. Lieutenant Delucchi's testimony about overhearing unidentified speakers making obscene threats should never have been allowed on the record.

In May 1945, Secretary Forrestal's office sent a memo to Admiral Wright, telling him the court had made a mistake. Admiral Osterhaus and the other judges would have to reconsider their decision, but without the evidence that should not have been admitted.

Osterhaus and the other officers met in early June. They voted to uphold all fifty convictions and prison sentences.

In July, Marshall got a letter from the Navy telling him the appeal had been rejected. "The trials were conducted fairly and impartially," the Judge Advocate General's office concluded. "Racial discrimination was guarded against."

"It is shocking, to say the least," a furious Marshall protested in a letter to Forrestal. "I have never run across a prosecutor with a more definite racial bias than that exemplified by Lieutenant Commander Coakley."

He asked Forrestal for a face-to-face meeting to talk over the case. But it was a long shot, he knew.

"All the appeals were over," he later said of this low point.

Japan surrendered to the Allies on August 15, 1945. Americans celebrated an incredibly hard-fought victory in World War II. Soldiers and sailors started coming home.

For Joe Small and the other prisoners at Terminal Island, two more months passed with no update on their case from Secretary Forrestal.

Finally, on October 29, Marshall got a letter from Forrestal.

"I should be happy to confer with you about this case," read Marshall, "if I felt that any purpose would be served."

Forrestal had looked over the trial records, he assured Marshall. He'd considered carefully the concerns Marshall raised. None of it changed his mind.

"I do not feel that any purpose would be served by a further presentation."

The legal process was dead.

SMALL GOES TO SEA

MUCH TO SECRETARY FORRESTAL'S irritation, the Port Chicago story lived on.

People kept sending in petitions demanding justice. A few members of Congress began making noises about the need for an investigation. Lester Granger continued reporting on the integration process. The effort was going well, he told Forrestal, but if the Navy wanted to show black servicemen it was really serious about change, one convincing step would be to free the Port Chicago sailors.

Eleanor Roosevelt was following the case too. Without telling Forrestal how to do his job, she made her position clear by sending him a copy of the NAACP's persuasive pamphlet, with a hand-written note attached.

"I hope in the case of these boys special care will be taken."

Feeling the pressure, Forrestal privately reconsidered the case. The Port Chicago sailors had been handed harsh sentences, he knew, largely to send a message about the dangers of defying orders during wartime. With the war won, those sentences looked a bit extreme.

Forrestal still wasn't about to admit the Navy had made a mistake in convicting the men of mutiny. But maybe he could make the whole controversy quietly disappear.

In the first week of January 1946, Joe Small was in his cell at Terminal Island when an officer came through shouting orders he'd heard only in dreams.

"Pack your bags! You're shippin' out!"

The officer didn't say when, didn't say where. That evening, Small and the other Port Chicago prisoners were marched out of the prison, loaded onto trucks, and driven to a nearby pier. Separated into groups of five or six, each was marched up the gangplank of a Navy ship.

Small carried his bag of clothes to a cabin. He lay in a bunk and went to sleep. He still had no idea what was going on.

Waking the next morning to the unfamiliar feel of rolling and pitching, he climbed up to the deck and was shocked to see only ocean in all directions. He turned to a sailor standing nearby.

"How far are we from the nearest land?"

"About two miles," the guy said.

Small looked around, saw nothing but blue. "Which way?"

"Straight down."

The men looked at each other for a moment—and both burst out laughing.

On January 7, 1946—a couple days after the Port Chicago men had left land—the Secretary of Navy's office made it official. The convicted mutineers had been released from prison and returned to active duty for service at sea. Why the secrecy and the delayed announcement? It was all part of Forrestal's plan to dispose of the story as quietly as possible.

But aboard Small's ship, the arrival of five of the famous Port Chicago mutineers was big news. "There was plenty of curiosity," Small remembered. The white sailors wanted to know all the details of what had *really* happened at Port Chicago.

"When they heard what we'd been through, they said they'd have done the same thing."

If the Navy truly believed these men were guilty of mutiny in time of war, why let them off with the light punishment of just sixteen months in jail? And if the Navy really considered the men dangerous mutineers, why send them to sea aboard ships?

Forrestal never answered these questions, probably because the decision to free the men made absolutely no sense—not unless the Navy considered the mutiny convictions to have been a mistake in the first place. Navy officials were not willing to admit this. The Port Chicago fifty were given the chance to finish their naval service as free men.

But they remained convicted mutineers.

Meanwhile, the Navy continued knocking down walls. At the end of World War II, the Navy announced plans to end segregation at all of its training camps. And in February 1946, just a month after the Port Chicago prisoners were let out of jail, the Navy became the first branch of the U.S. military to officially eliminate all racial barriers.

"Effective immediately," stated the historic order, "all restrictions governing types of assignments for which Negro personnel are eligible are hereby lifted. Henceforth they shall be eligible for all types of assignments in all ratings in all activities and all ships of the naval service."

The Navy's decision to end segregation led to an even bigger change. Impressed by the progress being made in the Navy, President Harry Truman issued Executive Order 9981 in July 1948.

"Whereas it is essential that there be maintained in the armed services of the United States the highest standards of democracy, with equality of treatment and opportunity for all those who serve in our country's defense," the now-famous order began, "it is hereby declared to be the policy of the President that there shall be equality of treatment and opportunity for all persons in the armed services without regard to race, color, religion or national origin."

Truman's order to end segregation in all branches of the United States military was only the beginning of the struggle against segregation in the United States. "We have just begun to scratch the surface in the fight," Thurgood Marshall cautioned.

But still, desegregation of the military was a serious start. It was a major step forward for the country, and a spark of inspiration for the massive civil rights movement still to come.

Joe Small's experience at sea offered a perfect preview of the enormous challenges—and enormous potential—that lay ahead for Americans.

"I was the first black seaman that a lot of these white fellows ever saw," Small recalled. "I had a lot of conflict over that."

The tensions burst open one day in the mess hall, when a gigantic redhead from Alabama named Alex set his tray down across the table from Small.

"By gawd," the young man bellowed, "this is the first time I ever ate with a nigger!"

Small lifted his cup of coffee and dashed the liquid in the

redhead's face. Then he hit the guy with the empty mug. Then he dove over the table onto him.

"I mean we tore up that dining room," Small said of the furious fight that followed. Small was a wiry 150 pounds; the Alabaman was six-three, 260. But Small used his speed to keep things close. "I was so fast he couldn't hit me. He was so hard I couldn't hurt him. We both got dog-tired."

Finally, the captain shoved his way through the cheering sailors and pulled the men apart.

"You wanna fight," the captain grunted, "put on boxing gloves and go out on the fantail."

So the men put on gloves and continued the bout on the back of the deck, with everyone watching. The big man swung hard, but couldn't connect. Small landed a few punches, but with no apparent effect.

After a few minutes, they were too tired to go on.

The skipper stepped in. "All right, knock it off," he said. "Shake hands."

Small reached out his hand. Alex took it. And from that moment on, they were best friends.

"Everywhere I went," said Small, "he was with me."

On shore leave in San Francisco, they'd hit the bars together.

"Gimme two beers!" Small's friend would call.

Often, the bartender would glance at the two sailors, one white and one black, and set down a single beer in front of the white sailor. When that happened, Alex would slide the glass to Small.

Then he'd glare over the bar and growl, "Now give *me* a beer."

If the bartender so much as hesitated, Alex would leap over the bar, grab a glass, and help himself. Then he'd leap back and lean on the bar beside Small, and the two friends would sip their beers together.

During one of their many conversations, Small asked Alex what it was that had caused him to change his mind about befriending a black man.

"I found out something," the big redhead said to Small. "A man is a man."

EPILOGUE: CIVIL RIGHTS HEROES

THINGS WERE DEFINITELY beginning to change.

In early July 1944—just ten days before the explosion at Port Chicago—a young black officer, Lieutenant Jack Robinson, had boarded a bus at Fort Hood, Texas. The white driver told Robinson to move farther back; Robinson refused. The furious driver called for the military police. Robinson and the MPs had an angry confrontation, and Robinson wound up facing a court-martial, charged with insubordination. He was found not guilty. It was such a typical case in World War II, hardly anyone noticed.

Less than three years later, everyone noticed Robinson. On April 15, 1947, at Ebbets Field in Brooklyn, New York, Jack Robinson—Jackie to his teammates—took the field as the starting first baseman for the Brooklyn Dodgers. It was a rocky road, being the first black player in Major League Baseball. Some opposing players barked racist filth at him when he came up to bat; some even tried to slice open his legs with flying spikes.

But in American history, change is never smooth, never without resistance.

Jackie Robinson became the first African American player in Major League Baseball.

In 1948 President Truman issued his historic order ending segregation in the military. Again, not everyone accepted the new reality. Port Chicago veteran Spencer Sikes saw this up close when he reenlisted in the Navy in 1951, during the Korean War.

"Things had changed," Sikes said of conditions on his integrated ship, "but to some degree, the people that were in command, they hadn't changed." The military, to its credit, pushed integration forward. By the time the Korean War ended in 1953, 95 percent of African American servicemen were serving in integrated units.

Meanwhile, Thurgood Marshall kept on challenging segregation in court—and kept on winning. In the landmark case of

Brown v. Board of Education of Topeka, Kansas, Marshall argued that segregation of public schools violated the constitutional rights of black children. In a 9–0 ruling in 1954, the Supreme Court agreed.

A year later, in Montgomery, Alabama, Rosa Parks was arrested for refusing to give up her seat to a white passenger on a public bus. A young pastor, Dr. Martin Luther King, Jr., helped lead a boycott of city buses, bringing national attention to the injustice of segregation.

These are the stories we think of as the foundation of the civil rights movement, and rightfully so. But it's important to remember that before *Brown v. Board of Education* or Truman's executive order, before Rosa Parks or Jackie Robinson—before any of this, there was Port Chicago.

Unlike Jackie Robinson or Rosa Parks, the young sailors from Port Chicago are not remembered as heroes. After finishing their military service, the men returned home and quietly got on with their lives.

Percy Robinson was among the sailors who agreed to go back to work after Admiral Wright's "death will be the penalty" speech on the baseball diamond. He served at sea, was honorably discharged from the Navy, and had a successful career as an environmental engineer in Los Angeles.

Robert Routh, the sailor blinded in the Port Chicago blast, earned a master's degree in sociology, worked as a counselor for the Veterans Administration, and became president of the Blinded Veterans Association. Amazingly, Routh and Robinson attended the same Los Angeles church for years before realizing they'd served together as teenagers decades before.

"I never talked about my past much," Routh explained. "He didn't either."

That was typical of the Port Chicago survivors. Many of the men—especially those convicted of mutiny—kept the memories buried. It was the only way they could move forward with their lives.

For years, Freddie Meeks couldn't talk about what had happened. "It would hurt inside," he said thirty-five years after the war. "You didn't want your friends to know that you had been charged with mutiny, you didn't want people to think, you know, that you didn't like your country."

Albert Williams didn't even tell his wife or children about Port Chicago and the mutiny trial. "Every time I would bring it up, or even think about it, I got a hateful feeling," he said. "It would just about tear me apart."

Like the other convicted mutineers, Joe Small was discharged "under honorable conditions"—a category of discharge given to men who have performed their duty satisfactorily, but whose record contains some type of disciplinary action. The "honorable conditions" discharge meant Small was eligible for veterans' health care benefits, but not for the GI Bill, which paid college tuition for veterans. This was a significant disadvantage to a young man trying to start a new life.

Small moved back to New Jersey, married a woman he'd known before the war, and went into the construction business. He was able to earn a decent living building and repairing homes, but always felt the mutiny conviction hanging over him, limiting his opportunities.

"It branded me," he said, "as a person incapable of following orders."

Freddie Meeks in 1994, holding a picture of himself as a young sailor.

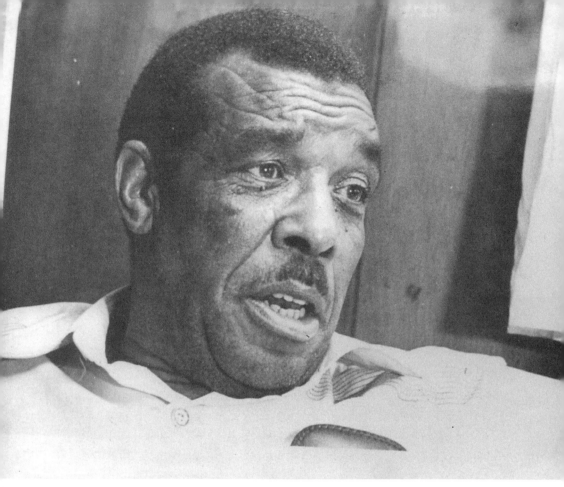

Joe Small

Small saw great changes in the country in the decades after World War II—but saw plenty of room for improvement too. He always hired crews with both white and black workers, for example. And without fail, whenever salesmen or bank officials came to one of Small's construction sites, they'd approach one of the white men first.

"You're Mr. Small?" they'd ask.

"No," the worker would say, pointing. "That's Mr. Small standing alongside of you."

Small would smile to himself, watching the visitor's face flush red at having assumed the boss had to be white.

Incredibly, in spite of everything, Joe Small never looked back on his wartime experience with bitterness. "I didn't have so hard a time that I carry a grudge against the Navy," he said.

Robert Routh, too, chose to focus on the positive. "I'm glad that I have lived long enough now to see the path of the nation has changed to the degree that it has."

Percy Robinson put it best. "I feel that the country at the time was ignorant," he said, looking back to the 1940s. "They did what they thought was best, which was stupid. And I forgave them for being stupid."

In the decades after the war, Port Chicago veterans and their families worked to overturn the convictions of the fifty men.

Robert Edwards, who was wounded in the Port Chicago explosion, was in the hospital when the other men were ordered to return to loading ammunition. He wasn't among the fifty who refused to go back—but always knew he could have been, if not for his wounds. After the war, Edwards helped the NAACP in its campaign to convince the Navy to reconsider the case. But the Navy saw Port Chicago as ancient history, and had no interest in reopening the files.

"It's like trying to fight a stone wall," Edwards said of the effort.

A University of California, Berkeley, professor named Robert Allen gave the effort a huge push forward. Allen spent years tracking down and interviewing men who'd served at Port Chicago, including many of the convicted mutineers. If not for Allen's tireless cross-country treks, the stories of these men, told in their

own words, would have been lost forever. His 1989 book, *The Port Chicago Mutiny*, sparked fresh press coverage of the case and documentary films about what had happened at Port Chicago and Mare Island.

This moved several members of Congress from California to petition the secretary of the Navy to review the cases of the convicted mutineers. The secretary wrote back saying it was too late to reexamine cases from World War II, but that the men were free to apply to the President of the United States for pardons.

The Constitution grants the president the power to pardon anyone convicted of a crime in federal or military court. A presidential pardon can get a person out of prison, but does not erase the conviction from his record. For many of the Port Chicago fifty, including Joe Small, this was not good enough.

"We don't want a pardon," Small said, "because that means, 'You're guilty but we forgive you.' We want the decisions set aside."

Representative George Miller, whose district includes Port Chicago, continued pressing the Navy to review the case. Finally, naval officials agreed.

The Navy finished its review in 1994, conceding in its report that, "racial discrimination did play a part in the assignment of African-American sailors to load ammunition [at Port Chicago], and that African-American sailors were subjected to segregated living and working conditions."

The report went on to conclude, however, that "racial prejudice and discrimination played no part in the court-martial convictions or sentences, and that there was nothing unfair or unjust in the final outcome of any of the Port Chicago court-martials."

Robert Edwards in 2004, holding a picture of himself as a young sailor.

The mutiny convictions stood.

Joe Small died in 1996, at the age of seventy-five.

Freddie Meeks, who was in declining health, decided it was time to seek a presidential pardon, if only to keep the story alive for future generations. "After all these years, the world should know what happened at Port Chicago," he said.

Another of the surviving fifty, Jack Crittenden, decided not to ask for a presidential pardon, explaining that he refused to ask forgiveness for a crime he didn't commit.

In December 1999, President Bill Clinton signed a pardon for Freddie Meeks.

"I knew God was keeping me around for something," Meeks told a newspaper reporter. "But I'm sorry so many of the others are not around to see it."

Family members and activists are still working to convince the Navy to exonerate the men, but it's far from certain the Navy will ever agree to reopen the case.

All of the Port Chicago fifty have died.

All fifty remain convicted mutineers.

Was it worth it?

The men from Port Chicago had the rest of their lives to ponder this question. Looking back at the events of 1944 from the distance of old age, the men could see that they'd played a key role in ending segregation in the military. But that had to be balanced against the heavy price they'd paid for defying authority.

"I think it was worth the effort," Percy Robinson concluded.

Percy Robinson poses with his military journal on July 20, 2007.

"It was worth the effort, showing that whatever you believe in, you at least tried to back it, the best you knew how."

"Well, I don't know whether it was right or wrong," said Freddie Meeks. "Maybe we shouldn't have," he began, since, after all, they were sailors in the U.S. Navy and had a duty to obey orders. "But then again," he reasoned, "maybe we *should*—to try to bring out the wrongs in the Navy, the way they treated us, the way they treated the blacks at that time."

Martin Bordenave never second-guessed his refusal to return to loading ammunition after the Port Chicago explosion. "I'm glad I did it, you know. I feel that I did something for the black race."

Bordenave knew there were no statues of the Port Chicago fifty—he and the others were not seen as civil rights heroes by the nation. It was enough for him to know he'd helped to make the country a better place for his children and grandchildren. "Everything we've gotten, we've fought and suffered for," he said. "You gotta holler loud, you know."

Joe Small had decades to think about that decisive moment at Mare Island, when he'd gotten the "Column left" command. But no matter how many times he relived the scene, he couldn't see responding to Lieutenant Delucchi's orders any other way.

"If I had consented to go back to duty, I would not only be betraying myself, I would've been betraying them," Small said of other men of his division.

"I was fighting for something," he added. "Things were not right, and it was my desire to make things right. I have never felt ashamed of the decisions that I made. I did what I thought was best, and I did it in the best way I knew how."

SOURCE NOTES

My goal with this book was to tell the Port Chicago story largely from the point of view of the participants—the young sailors. This could not have been done without a set of oral histories of the men collected by Dr. Robert Allen in the late 1970s. With a combination of relentless detective work and an unlimited-mileage Greyhound bus ticket, Allen tracked down Joseph Small and many of the other Port Chicago sailors, crisscrossing the country to record their stories. Allen generously shared those interviews with me, and they are by far the most important sources for this book.

Also key are other interviews of the Port Chicago sailors done for books, articles, documentaries, and radio programs. The court-martial chapters are based largely on the trial transcript, a 1,400 page document I was able to acquire on a single CD by filing a Freedom of Information Act request with the Navy. To fill in additional background information, I relied on dozens of books, articles, and government records. Below are the sources for the quotes and other details included in this book, organized by chapter.

First Hero

1 Dorie Miller biographical information was found in: "Dorie Miller," *Ebony*, 132–133; Miller, *Messman*, 286.
1 "Japanese are attacking": "Reports by Survivors of Pearl Harbor

Attack, USS *West Virginia*." Online document collection. Washington, DC: Department of the Navy, Naval History & Heritage Command. http://www.history.navy.mil/docs/wwii/pearl/survivors.htm

2 Miller's Pearl Harbor action is described in: "Dorie Miller," *Ebony*, 132–133; Miller, *Messman*, 286–292; Reddick, *Negro in the U.S. Navy*, 204.

2 "It wasn't hard": US Navy, "Cook Third Class Doris Miller, USN." Online exhibit about Doris "Dorie" Miller. Washington, DC: Department of the Navy, Naval History & Heritage Command. http://www.history.navy.mil/faqs/faq57-4.htm

2 "Abandon ship": US Navy, "Reports by Survivors of Pearl Harbor Attack."

2 "For distinguished devotion": US Navy, "Cook Third Class."

4 "This marks the first time": US Navy, "Cook Third Class."

4 Navy's segregation policy: Nalty, *Strength for the Fight*, 186–190; MacGregor, *Integration*, 58–67.

The Policy

6 "We are now fighting": Address of President Franklin D. Roosevelt, delivered by radio from the White House, December 9, 1941. President Franklin D. Roosevelt Presidential Library and Museum. http://docs.fdrlibrary.marist.edu/firesi90.html

6 "Patriotic, red-blooded": Reddick, *Negro in the U.S. Navy*, 207.

7 For background on African Americans in U.S. wars, see: Dalfiume, *Desegregation*, 5–21; Nichols, *Breakthrough,* 23–32; MacGregor, *Integration*, 3–8.

9 "Poor Negroes": Dalfiume, *Desegregation*, 14.

9 "This policy has proven": Dalfiume, *Desegregation*, 39.

9 Information on Secretary Knox and the Navy's segregation policy was found in: MacGregor, *Integration*, 58–66.

11 "To go the whole way": MacGregor, *Integration*, 64.

11 A description of the Navy's new policy was found in: MacGregor, *Integration*, 58–66.

11 "In its abrupt announcement": *The Crisis*, May 1942, 161.

11 "It is difficult": *The Crisis*, May 1942, 161.

12 "All our men are facing": Crittenden interview.

12 "The feeling was": Robinson interview.

12 "We felt patriotic": "Port Chicago 50" radio broadcast.

13 "If you sign for me": Routh interview.

13 "What branch of the service": Small interview.

15 "You give me your axe": Small interview.

15 "Small, you have natural": Small interview.

Port Chicago

16 "We were so young": Routh interview.

16 "Most of us": Robinson interview.

16 "The first thing": Jameson interview.

16 "There were two lines": Robinson interview.

18 Details about the black-only training camp were found in: Allen, *Port Chicago*, 30–31; MacGregor, *Integration*, 67–68.

18 A description of the military's blood segregation policy was found in: Dalfiume, *Desegregation*, 107.

20 "Negro sailors": Edwards interview.

20 "When I first enlisted": Bordenave interview.

20 "See, when I come": Sheppard interview.

20 "Most of us": "Port Chicago 50" radio broadcast.

21 "We had expectations": Frank Productions, *Port Chicago Mutiny*.

21 A description of Port Chicago and its surroundings is found in: Allen, *Port Chicago*, 38–40; I was able to visit the still-active military base in July 2011.

21 "Strange thing": Routh interview.

21 "Big open place": Robinson interview.

21 "Dumpy looking place": "Port Chicago 50" radio broadcast.

23 "Most of the men obtainable": Allen, *Port Chicago*, 42.

24 "Ship us anywhere": Routh interview.

24 "The first time I saw": "Port Chicago 50" radio broadcast.

24 A description of officers being trained to work with explosives is found in: Allen, *Port Chicago*, 41.

24 "They just brought you": Meeks interview.

24 "I didn't know": Soublet interview.

25 The detail of civilian stevedores offering training is found in: Allen, *Port Chicago*, 42.

25 "Boy, I'll never make it": Sikes interview.

Work and Liberty

26 "All right, buddy": Small interview.

27 "My father didn't believe": Small interview.

27 "You think you can move": Small interview.

28 "You got a license": Small interview.

28 "I put a good whipping": Small interview.

29 "I demanded": Small interview.

29 Delucchi background is described in: Allen, *Port Chicago*, 96.

29 "Now hear this": Allen, *Port Chicago*, 2.

29 "He looked like": Robinson interview.

29 "He spent half the day": Sheppard interview.

29 "Very hot-tempered": Small interview.

30 Working conditions on the Port Chicago pier are described in many of the interviews, and in: Allen, *Port Chicago*, 46–49.

32 "We'd open the boxcar": Small interview.

32 "You'd hear this": "Port Chicago 50" radio broadcast.

33 "And that would": "Port Chicago 50" radio broadcast.

33 "Oh, no, don't worry": "Port Chicago 50" radio broadcast.

34 "Won't concussion blow": Small interview.

34 "You'd build yourself": Allen, *Port Chicago*, 47.

34 "We were all afraid": Small interview.

36 "Hey! Where's the winchman": Small interview.

36 "So whenever they needed": Small interview.

36 "He should have been": Sheppard interview.

36 "Look, you got a petty": Small interview.

37 "And that just put": Small interview.

37 "It was just a one-street": Routh interview.

37 "Other streets we were": Small interview.

38 "Let's go over": Frank Productions, *Port Chicago Mutiny*.

38 "What happened": Frank Productions, *Port Chicago Mutiny*.

38 "Where's the freedom": Edwards interview.

The Lawyer

39 "Here on the post": McGuire, *Taps*, 64.

39 Stories of segregation on American military bases were found in: McGuire, *Taps*, 11–27; Morehouse, *Jim Crow Army*, 94–109; *The Crisis*, April 1943, 116–118.

40 Trimmingham's letter to *YANK* is printed in: *Best from YANK*, 212–213.

42 Marshall biographical information and childhood stories were found in: Columbia: Marshall Oral History; Ball, *Defiant Life*, 13–17; Williams, *Thurgood Marshall*, 15–24.

42 "I gave them someplace": Marshall interview.

42 Rieves Bell story, including, "Where'd you get that": James, *Root and Branch*, 180.

43 "Don't push in front:" Williams, *Thurgood Marshall*, 15.

43 "Anyone calls you": Ball, *Defiant Life*, 17.

44 "It was worth it": Williams, *Thurgood Marshall*, 16.

44 "Before I left": Ball, *Defiant Life*, 18.

44 Marshall's war-time work is described in: Ball, *Defiant Life*, 55–69; Williams, *Thurgood Marshall*, 122–129.

45 The Nora Green story was found in: White, *A Man Called White*, 222.

45 The Edward Green story was found in: Long, *Marshalling Justice*, 133.

46 "I hope you can realize": Long, *Marshalling Justice*, 133.

46 "The urgency of the war": Dalfiume, *Desegregation*, 84.

46 "Negro soldiers are damned": *The Crisis*, September 1944, 289.

46 "Things are slowly coming": McGuire, *Taps*, 72.

Hot Cargo

47 "I have never felt": Allen, *Port Chicago*, 44.

47 "It was as fast": Robinson interview.

47 "It was pressure": "Port Chicago 50" radio broadcast.

47 "Efforts were made": *Record of Proceedings of a Court of Inquiry*, 6.

48 "We were pushed": Small interview.

48 "If he decided": Chronicle Broadcasting, *Port Chicago Mutiny*.

49 "I think in the minds": Sikes interview.

50 "There was no discrimination": *Record of Proceedings of a Court of Inquiry*, 7.

50 "We used to talk": Bordenave interview.

50 "You didn't see": Gay interview.

50 "Damn, man": Sheppard interview.

52 "You had ten, twelve guys": Robinson interview.

53 "How are things going": Small interview.

53 Port Chicago Personnel: Allen, *Port Chicago*, 46.

53 "The 17th of July": Routh interview.

53 Albert Carr story and quotes: Allen, *Port Chicago*, 27.

54 "Sikes! Telephone!": Sikes interview.

55 Ships at Port Chicago pier: Allen, *Port Chicago*, 56.

57 "Operations were proceeding": *Record of Proceedings of a Court of Inquiry*, 16.

57 "I had pimples": "Port Chicago 50" radio broadcast.

57 "But naturally that never": Small interview.

The Explosion

58 "Oh my God": Chronicle Broadcasting, *Port Chicago Mutiny*.

58 "The sky lit up": Chronicle Broadcasting, *Port Chicago Mutiny*.

58 "All these tremendous": Routh interview.

58 "It was like someone": Gay interview.

58 "My left arm": Robinson interview.

59 "Men were screaming": Sheppard interview.

59 "First thing I thought": "Port Chicago 50" radio broadcast.
59 "Get out of the barracks": "Port Chicago 50" radio broadcast.
59 "Hey! Come and get me": "Port Chicago 50" radio broadcast.
59 "And then darkness": Allen, *Port Chicago*, 61.
60 "It seemed to me": Allen, *Port Chicago*, 63.
60 Details about the Port Chicago movie theater are from: Allen, *Port Chicago*, 65.
61 "We hadn't been sitting": Rich interview.
62 "All military personnel": Sikes interview.
62 "What happened?": Jameson interview.
62 "There was no appearance": Allen, *Port Chicago*, 61.
62 "Fellows were cut": Small interview.
62 "I want to volunteer": "Port Chicago 50" radio broadcast.
63 "Go on down!": Sheppard interview.

The Inquiry

64 "And the right eye": "Port Chicago 50" radio broadcast.
64 The extensive damage to the base is described in: Allen, *Port Chicago*, 65–66; articles in *Oakland Tribune*, *People's World*, *New York Times*.
67 "Man, it was awful": Crittenden interview.
67 "Very seldom you'd find": Jameson interview.
68 "As we walked": "Blast at Port Chicago," *People's World*, July 19, 1944.
68 "We wouldn't want to go": "Blast at Port Chicago," *People's World*, July 19, 1944.
69 "Their sacrifice could not": "At Least 350 Dead," *New York Times*, July 19, 1944.
69 Court of Inquiry details were taken from: Allen, *Port Chicago*, 68–72; Navy's *Record of Proceedings of a Court of Inquiry*.
71 "The consensus of opinion": Allen, *Port Chicago*, 70.
71 "We had no idea": Small interview.
71 "You knew all of these": Sikes interview.
72 "I just don't believe": Meeks interview.

73 "Everybody was scared": Allen, *Port Chicago*, 72.

73 "It made a '*RRRRR*'": Small interview.

73 Compensation bill: Allen, *Port Chicago*, 67.

73 "What did they die for?": "Port Chicago Heroes," *Pittsburgh Courier*, August 5, 1944.

75 Purdie Jackson's story can be found in: Sullivan, *Lift Every Voice*, 272.

75 "We must not be delayed": Sullivan, *Lift Every Voice*, 295.

76 "The only thing we knew": Small interview.

76 "Put me on a ship": Allen, *Port Chicago*, 73.

76 "I was instrumental": Small interview.

76 "If these are for handling": Allen, *Port Chicago*, 80.

77 "What you gonna do?": Sheppard interview.

77 "I was a winch operator": Small interview.

77 "So I came to the conclusion": Small interview.

Column Left

78 "Division Four, turn to": Testimony of Ernest Delucchi, Trial Transcript, 40.

78 "There was a bit of milling": Testimony of Ernest Delucchi, Trial Transcript, 40.

80 "Okay, move 'em out": Small interview.

80 "Column left": Small interview.

80 "Will you go back": Small interview.

80 "Oh no we ain't": Robinson interview.

81 "Small, will you return": Terkel, *The Good War*, 396.

81 "What's the trouble?": Testimony of Jefferson Flowers, Trial Transcript, 103.

81 "We told him": Gay interview.

82 "You can fight back": Allen, *Port Chicago*, 99.

82 "You men have given me": Testimony of Ernest Delucchi, Trial Transcript, 45.

82 "You have been ordered": Testimony of Joseph Tobin, Trial Transcript, 18.

83 "You know, all this stuff": Robinson interview.

83 "I order you to load": Testimony of Carleton Morehouse, Trial Transcript, 113.

84 "Many men from the other": Testimony of James Tobin, Trial Transcript, 122.

84 "Anthony, how about it?": Testimony of Douglas Anthony, Trial Transcript, 419.

85 "Jack, now you're a fine": Crittenden interview.

85 Summary of day, numbers involved: Allen, *Port Chicago*, 82.

Prison Barge

87 "We were packed": Small interview.

87 "We were all scared": Crittenden interview.

87 "Two men would get": Small interview.

88 "There's no rule": Small interview.

88 "I saw spoons": Small interview.

88 "Now, the slightest provocation": Small interview.

88 "It was a pretty hairy situation": Small interview.

88 "All right fellows": Small interview.

89 "We were stubborn": Robinson interview.

89 "Improve working conditions": Small interview.

90 "Something's up": Small interview.

90 "Just in case you don't know": Allen, *Port Chicago*, 85.

91 "But what you going to do?": Robinson interview.

91 "He can't be telling": Robinson interview.

91 "I've got a wife": Crittenden interview.

91 "How could it be": Bordenave interview.

91 "Man, this guy can't": Crittenden interview.

91 "I have been ordered": Testimony of Ernest Delucchi, Trial Transcript, 62.

92 "I concentrated": Small interview.

92 "We didn't even know": Robinson interview.

92 "You gonna let them shoot": Gay interview.

The Fifty

93 "The admiral wants to talk": Small interview.

93 "Small, you are the leader": Small interview.

93 "You bald-headed son": Small interview.

94 "That branded me": Small interview.

94 "Go on brothers": Routh interview.

94 "Small, how do you feel": Chronicle Broadcasting, *Port Chicago Mutiny*.

94 "I, for one": Small interview.

94 "An unlawful opposition": Statement of Gerald Veltmann, pg. 1, printed with Trial Transcript.

95 "There are undoubtedly": Report from Commanding Officer Goss, pg. 2, printed with Trial Transcript.

95 "The refusal to perform": Admiral Wright report to Secretary Forrestal, pg. 2, printed with Trial Transcript.

97 "They were activated": Allen, *Port Chicago*, 91.

97 FDR passes note to Eleanor: Allen, *Port Chicago*, 91.

97 "conspired each with the other": Official Charge, Trial Transcript, 2.

97 Background information on James Coakley was found in: Allen, *Port Chicago*, 92.

97 "Small was supposed": Waldrop interview.

99 "Well, somebody has got to be": Waldrop interview.

99 "Jack, I'm here to help": Crittenden interview.

99 "I didn't say the things": Crittenden interview.

100 Bannon-Small interview, beginning, "How was it that the men": The record of this interview was read at the court-martial trial, Testimony of Joseph Small, Trial Transcript, 389.

101 "It wasn't discussed": Small interview.

101 Coakley's investigation is described in: Allen, *Port Chicago*, 87–88.

102 Gerald Veltmann background information comes from: Allen, *Port Chicago*, 92.

102 "I figured we'd go": Bordenave, interview.

103 "Oh I would say": Chronicle Broadcasting, *Port Chicago Mutiny*.

Treasure Island

104 Details of the courtroom setting and interior are found in: Allen, *Port Chicago*, 93; "Paradox in Mutiny Trial," *People's World,* October 28, 1944.

105 "You have heard the charge": Statement of James Coakley, Trial Transcript, 4.

105 Testimony of Commander Joseph Tobin: Trial Transcript, 14–36.

110 Testimony of Lieutenant Ernest Delucchi: Trial Transcript, 36–89.

Prosecution

114 "We concede the fact": "No Conspiracy to Mutiny," *California Eagle,* Sept. 21, 1944.

114 "The Negro people are well aware": "Trial of Negro Sailors Begins," *People's World,* September 18, 1944.

114 James Forrestal's point of view and plans for change are discussed in: MacGregor, *Integration,* 84; Granger, "Racial Democracy," 61–62.

115 "Admiral, I'd like to make a change": Nichols, *Breakthrough,* 62.

116 Testimony of Edward Johnson: Trial Transcript, 165.

116 The reporter's description of Coakley comes from: "Murder Threat in Navy Trial," *People's World,* October 5, 1944.

117 Testimony of Joseph Gray: Trial Transcript, 233–234.

118 Testimony of Edward Stubblefield, Trial Transcript, 186–190.

121 "Did anybody ever try": Testimony of John Thompson, Trial Transcript, 249–250.

122 The detail of the judges nodding off is found in: Allen, *Port Chicago,* 104; "Paradox in Mutiny Trial," *People's World,* October 28, 1944.

122 "There is no sufficient evidence": Long, *Marshalling Justice,* 141.

Joe Small

123 Testimony of Joseph Small: Trial Transcript, 365–406.
127 Years after the trial, Small described Veltmann's advice in his interview with Robert Allen: Small interview.
130 "Defense counsel are good": Williams, *Thurgood Marshall*, 126.
131 "I'm Thurgood Marshall": Sheppard interview.
131 "He just said to play it cool": Meeks interview.
131 "The defense strategy": Bordenave interview.
131 "The guy who was defending": Waldrop interview.
131 "I discussed it with them": Small interview.
131 "We couldn't volunteer": Small interview.
132 "That was the atmosphere": "Port Chicago 50" radio broadcast.

The Verdict

133 Testimony of John Dunn: Trial Transcript, 348–364.
134 Testimony of Julius Dixson: Trial Transcript, 650–659.
134 Testimony of Ollie Green: Trial Transcript, 326–348; Green's unsolicited "I got a couple of things to say" testimony is on 348.
135 The reaction to Green's unexpected testimony is described in: Allen, *Port Chicago*, 109.
136 Testimony of Frank Henry: Trial Transcript, 990–1011.
137 Testimony of Alphonso McPherson: Trial Transcript, 683–695.
138 "Lose your head": Ball, *Defiant Life*, 67.
138 "The NAACP is going to": "NAACP Will Expose Jim Crow Set-Up," *People's World*, October 17, 1944.
139 "A Navy Department investigation": "Marshall Demands Navy Probe," *People's World*, October 19, 1944.
139 Coakley's closing argument: Trial Transcript, 1348–1376.
140 Veltmann's closing argument: Trial Transcript, 1377–1403.
141 The judges deliberated (and, presumably, ate lunch) from 11:55 a.m. to 1:15 p.m.: Trial Transcript, 1435.

Hard Labor

143   "My knees almost hit": Sheppard interview.

143   "The verdict was guilty": "Port Chicago 50" radio broadcast.

143   "Fifteen years": Crittenden interview.

143   "I tried to calm the men": Small interview.

144   A description of the men being taken to Terminal Island is found in: Allen, *Port Chicago*, 128.

144   "You can look all the way": Waldrop interview.

144   "Everything was rigged": Small interview.

144   Veltmann reported Osterhaus's "We're going to find them guilty" quote in a documentary decades after the trial: Chronicle Broadcasting, *Port Chicago Mutiny*.

144   "one of the worst frame-ups": Allen, *Port Chicago*, 130.

145   "Why is it that the only": Long, *Marshalling Justice*, 142.

145   Forrestal's response to Marshall is described in: Long, *Marshalling Justice*, 148.

146   "The assimilation": MacGregor, *Integration*, 85.

146   "Before we reached": Nichols, *Breakthrough*, 60.

146   "The Navy has denied them": NAACP pamphlet "Mutiny?" 11.

147   "Hard labor was anything": Terkel, *The Good War*, 398.

147   The Guam incident is described in: MacGregor, *Integration*, 92–93.

148   Information on the Camp Rousseau hunger strike was found in: Nelson, *The Integration*, 84.

148   Forrestal's push toward integration is described in: Allen, *Port Chicago*, 134–135; MacGregor, *Integration*, 94–95.

148   "The Navy accepts no theories": MacGregor, *Integration*, 84.

150   "We didn't socialize": Waldrop interview.

150   The text of Marshall's statement to the Navy appeal board is printed in the Trial Transcript. It is not assigned page numbers in the document, but is found toward the beginning, before the testimony begins.

152   The Navy's response to Marshall's appeal is described in the Trial Transcript, following Marshall's statement, and in Allen, *Port Chicago*, 133.

152   "The trials were conducted": Long, *Marshalling Justice*, 148.

152   "It is shocking": Long, *Marshalling Justice*, 148.

152 "All the appeals were over": Marshall interview.

152 "I should be happy to confer": Long, *Marshalling Justice*, 148.

Small Goes to Sea

153 Granger's report to Forrestal is described in: Allen, *Port Chicago*, 135; MacGregor, *Integration*, 96. For a detailed description of his work with the Navy, see: Granger, "Racial Democracy—The Navy Way" 61–66.

153 "I hope in the case": Roosevelt, Eleanor. Letter to James Forrestal, April 8, 1945. Records of the Navy, Correspondence Files of the Secretary of the Navy, James Forrestal.

154 "Pack your bags!" Small interview.

154 "How far are we": Small interview.

155 "There was plenty of curiosity": Small interview.

155 Navy ends segregation: Wollenberg, "Blacks vs. Navy Blue," 62–75.

156 Truman's Executive Order 9981: "Desegregation of the Armed Forces." Online timeline at the Harry S. Truman Library and Museum: http://www.trumanlibrary.org

156 "I was the first black seaman": Small interview.

156 Small described his his fight with Alex and subsequent friendship in: Small interview; Terkel, *The Good War*, 399–400.

Epilogue: Civil Rights Heroes

159 Jackie Robinson's military experience and court-martial is detailed in: Vernon, "Jim Crow, Meet Lieutenant Robinson," 36–43.

160 "Things had changed": Sikes interview.

163 "I never talked about my past": Chronicle Broadcasting, *Port Chicago Mutiny*.

163 "It would hurt inside": "Port Chicago 50" radio broadcast.

163 "Every time I would bring it up": "Port Chicago 50" radio broadcast.

163   "It branded me": "Port Chicago 50" radio broadcast.

165   "I didn't have so hard": Small interview.

165   "I'm glad that I have lived": Routh interview.

165   "I feel that the country": Chronicle Broadcasting, *Port Chicago Mutiny.*

165   Efforts to convince the Navy to reopen the case are summarized in: Allen, *Port Chicago*, 183–186.

165   "It's like trying to fight": Edwards interview.

167   "We don't want a pardon": "Navy Refuses to Reopen Court-Martial Cases," *San Francisco Chronicle,* August 22, 1990.

167   "racial discrimination did play a part": "Port Chicago 50" radio broadcast.

168   "After all these years": Allen, *Port Chicago*, 186.

168   For the story of Freddie Meeks receiving his pardon, see: "From Peril to Pardon," *Los Angeles Times,* December 24, 1999.

168   "I think it was worth the effort": Robinson interview.

170   "Well, I don't know": Meeks interview.

170   "I'm glad I did it": Bordenave interview.

170   "Everything we've gotten": Bordenave interview.

170   Small sums up: Small interview.

170   "I was fighting": "Port Chicago 50" radio broadcast.

LIST OF WORKS CITED

Books

Allen, Robert L. *The Port Chicago Mutiny: The Story of the Largest Mass Mutiny Trial in U.S. Naval History*. New York: Warner Books, 1989.

Ball, Howard. *A Defiant Life: Thurgood Marshall & the Persistence of Racism in America*. New York: Crown Publishers, 1998.

Bell, Christopher M. and Bruce Elleman, eds. *Naval Mutinies of the Twentieth Century: An International Perspective*. London: Frank Cass Publishers, 2003.

Buchanan, Russell A. *Black Americans in World War II*. Santa Barbara, CA: Clio Books, 1977.

Dalfiume, Richard, M. *Desegregation of the U.S. Armed Forces: Fighting on Two Fronts, 1939–1953*. Columbia, MO: University of Missouri Press, 1969.

Editors of Yank: *The Best from YANK the Army Weekly, 1945*. Cleveland, OH: World Pub., 1945.

Gerstle, Gary. *American Crucible: Race and Nation in the Twentieth Century*. Princeton, NJ: Princeton University Press, 2001.

James, Rawn, Jr. *Root and Branch: Charles Hamilton Houston, Thurgood Marshall, and the Struggle to End Segregation*. New York: Bloomsday Press, 2010.

Lash, Joseph P. *Eleanor and Franklin: The Story of Their Relationship Based on Eleanor Roosevelt's Private Papers*. New York: W.W. Norton & Company, 1971.

Long, Michael G., ed. *Marshalling Justice: The Early Civil Rights Letters*. New York: Amistad, 2011.

MacGregor, Morris J. *Integration of the Armed Forces*. Washington, D.C.: Center of Military History, United States Army, 1985.

McGuire, Phillip. *Taps for a Jim Crow Army: Letters from Black Soldiers in World War II*. Santa Barbara, CA: ABC-Clio, 1983.

Miller, Richard, E. *The Messman Chronicles: African Americans in the U.S. Navy, 1932–1943*. Annapolis, MD: Naval Institute Press, 2004.

Morehouse, Maggi M. *Fighting in the Jim Crow Army: Black Men and Women Remember World War II.* Lantham, MD: Rowman & Littlefield Publishers, 2000.

Nalty, Bernard, C. *Strength for the Fight: A History of Black Americans in the Military.* New York: The Free Press, 1989.

Nelson, Dennis. *The Integration of the Negro into the U.S. Navy.* New York: Farrar, Straus and Young, 1951.

Nichols, Lee. *Breakthrough on the Color Front.* New York: Random House, 1954.

Prange, Gordon W. *Dec 7, 1941: The Day the Japanese Attacked Pearl Harbor.* New York: McGraw-Hill Book Company, 1988.

Rampersad, Arnold and Rachel Robinson. *Jackie Robinson: A Biography.* New York: Random House, 1997.

Sullivan, Patricia. *Lift Every Voice: The NAACP and the Making of the Civil Rights Movement.* New York: New Press, 2009.

Terkel, Studs. *The Good War: An Oral History of World War Two.* New York: New Press, 1984.

Tushnet, Mark V. *Making Civil Rights Law: Thurgood Marshall and the Supreme Court, 1936–1961.* New York: Oxford University Press, 1994.

White, Walter. *A Man Called White: The Autobiography of Walter White.* New York: Viking Press, 1948.

Williams, Juan. *Thurgood Marshall: American Revolutionary.* New York: Three Rivers Press, 1998.

Articles & Pamphlets

"50 Navy Sentences Reported Voided," *New York Times*, January 7, 1946.

"50 Sailors Face Trial for Mutiny," *Chicago Defender*, September 23, 1944.

"83 Sailors Back on Duty; Forrestal Reinstated Negroes Convicted in Two Cases," *New York Times,* January 8, 1946.

"300 Die in Bay Arms Ship Blast," *Oakland Tribune*, July 18, 1944.

"Along the NAACP Battlefront," *The Crisis* (magazine of the NAACP), April 1943, 116–118.

"At Least 350 Dead As Munitions Ships Blow Up On Coast," *New York Times*, July 19, 1944.

"Believes Sailors Innocent of Charge," *Pittsburgh Courier*, November 4, 1944.

"Blast at Port Chicago," *People's World (San Francisco)*, July 19, 1944.

"Concussion Coincides with Movie Bomb Scene," *New York Times*, July 19, 1944.

"Defense Begins in Mutiny Trial of 50," *Chicago Defender*, October 7, 1944.

"Dorie Miller: First U.S. Hero of World War II," *Ebony*, December 1969, 132–138.

"Foul in Navy Trial?" *People's World*, October 27, 1944.

"Freddie Meeks, Pardoned in Port Chicago Mutiny," (obituary) *San Francisco Chronicle*, June 21, 2003.

"From Peril to Pardon: Clinton exonerates L.A. man, 80, convicted of mutiny after disaster," *Los Angeles Times*, December 24, 1999.

Granger, Lester B. "Racial Democracy—The Navy Way" *Common Ground*, Winter, 1947, 61–66.

"Marshall Demands Navy Probe," *People's World*, October 19, 1944.

"Marshall Represents Mutineers," *Pittsburgh Courier*, October 14, 1944.

Mays, Benjamin E. "The Negro and the Present War," *The Crisis,* May 1942, 160–165.

"Murder Threat in Navy Trial," *People's World*, October 5, 1944.

"Mutiny?: The real story of how the Navy branded 50 fear-shocked sailors as mutineers." Pamphlet published by the NAACP Legal Defense and Educational Fund, Inc., March 1945.

"Mutiny of 50 Sailors Told Court-Martial," *Oakland Tribune*, September 15, 1944.

"Mutiny Prosecutor Is Charged with Prejudice by Marshall," *California Eagle*, October 19, 1944.

"NAACP Asks Navy Dept. Probe of Mutiny Charge," *Pittsburgh Courier*, October 28, 1944.

"NAACP Will Expose Jim Crow Set-Up," *People's World*, October 17, 1944.

Nalty, Bernard, C. *The Right to Fight: African American Marines in World War II*. Booklet published by the U.S. Marine Corps History and Museums Division, 1995.

"Navy Board Begins Inquiry on Blast," *New York Times*, July 21, 1944.

"Navy Refuses to Reopen Court-Martial Cases," *San Francisco Chronicle*, August 22, 1990.

"Navy Trial Nears End," *People's World*, October 20, 1944.

"Negro Soldiers Convicted," *People's World*, October 25, 1944.

"No Conspiracy to Mutiny Says Navy Chaplain at Port Chicago," *California Eagle*, Sept. 21, 1944.

"Paradox in Mutiny Trial: Somebody Had to Take the Rap—The Guilty One Wasn't Even Tried," *People's World*, October 28, 1944.

"Port Chicago Heroes," *Pittsburgh Courier*, August 5, 1944.

"Port Chicago 'Mutiny' Trial of 50 Becoming 'Hot Potato' for Navy," *Chicago Defender*, October 21, 1944.

"Port Chicago Naval 'Mutiny' Trial On," *Oakland Tribune*, September 14, 1944.

"Port Chicago, site of a World War II home front tragedy, is a classroom today," *Los Angeles Times*, September 5, 2010.

Reddick, L. D. "The Negro in the United States Navy During World War II," *The Journal of Negro History*, Vol. 32, No. 2 (April 1947), 201–219.

Reynolds, Grant, U.S. Army chaplain, "1944: "What the Negro Soldier Thinks about This War," *The Crisis*, September 1944, 289–299.

Schubert, Frank N. "Buffalo Soldiers at San Juan Hill." Paper delivered by the author at the 1998 Conference of Army Historians in Bethesda, Maryland.

"Testimony Continues in Navy Trial," *People's World*, September 19, 1944.

"Torpedo Hit the *Arizona* First, Navy Men of Pearl Harbor Say," *New York Times*, December 22, 1941.

"Trial of Negro Sailors Begins," *People's World*, September 18, 1944.

Vernon, John. "Jim Crow, Meet Lieutenant Robinson: A 1944 Court-Martial." *Prologue*, publication of the National Archives, Spring 2008, 36–43.

"Witnesses Awed by Pyrotechnics," *New York Times*, July 19, 1944.

"Were Navy Trial Statements Fixed?" *People's World*, October 19, 1944.

Wollenberg, Charles. "Blacks vs. Navy Blue: The Mare Island Mutiny Court-martial," *California History*, Vol. 58, No. 1 (Spring 1979), 62–75.

Oral Histories & Documentaries

Bordenave, Martin. Interview by Robert Allen, August 23, 1980.

Boykin, Sammie L. Interview by Tracey Panek, Oral History Interview project for the Port Chicago Naval Magazine National Memorial, National Parks Service, August 14, 1999.

Crittenden, Jack. Interview by Robert Allen, July 22, 1980.

Edwards, Robert. Interview by Tracey Panek, March 10, 1995.

Gay, Willie. Interview by Robert Allen, December 14, 1977.

Jameson, DeWitt. Interview by Tracey Panek, August 13, 1999.

Meeks, Freddie. Interview by Robert Allen, August 24, 1980.

Port Chicago Mutiny documentary film. Frank Productions, Inc., for The Learning Channel, 1999.

Port Chicago Mutiny: A National Tragedy documentary film, Chronicle Broadcasting Company of San Francisco, 1990.

Reminiscences of Thurgood Marshall. Columbia University, Columbia Center for Oral History, New York, 1977.

Rich, Morris. Interview by Tracey Panek, July 17, 1999.

Robinson, Percy. Interview by Robert Allen, May 20, 1978.

Routh, Robert. Interview by Robert Allen, May 21, 1978.

Sheppard, Cyril. Interview by Robert Allen, October 20, 1977.

Sikes, Spencer E. Interview by Tracey Panek, November 11, 1995.

Small, Joseph R. Interviews by Robert Allen, September 6, 1977; June 3, 1978; June 10, 1978.

Soublet, Morris J., Sr. Interview by Tracey Panek, April 10, 1999.

Tenger, Harold A., Interview by Tracey Panek, July 30, 1999.

"The Port Chicago 50: An Oral History," Radio Program, broadcast on *This American Life* in 1996.

Waldrop, Edward. Interview by Robert Allen, December 9, 1977.

Wiley, Duane F. Interview by Tracey Panek, March 9, 2000.

U.S. Navy Records

"Commanding Officer Praises Negro Personnel Who Served at Port Chicago After Explosion Monday Night," U.S. Navy. Press and Radio Release, 20 Jul. 1944.

"Guide to Command of Negro Naval Personnel." Pamphlet published for the information and guidance of all Naval officers. Navy Department, Bureau of Naval Personnel, 12 February 1945.

"Record of Proceedings of a Court of Inquiry Convened at the U.S. Naval Magazine, Port Chicago, California," July 21, 1944. Navy Judge Advocate General's Office, Washington, D.C.

Trial Transcript, General Court-Martial, "Case of Julius J. Allen, Seaman Second Class, U.S. Naval Reserve, et al.," September 14–October 24, 1944. Navy Judge Advocate General's Office, Washington, D.C.

Acknowledgments

First off, thanks to my brother-in-law, Eric Person, who first brought this story to my attention. While I was researching a previous book, *Bomb* (on the race to make the first atomic bomb), Eric asked if I'd heard the theory that the first atomic test was not in the New Mexico desert in July 1945, as recorded in history, but a year earlier at a California naval base called Port Chicago. Intrigued, I looked into it. Basically, the speculation is that the July 1944 disaster at Port Chicago was not an accidental munitions blast—supposedly it was an atomic bomb, part of a top-secret government test of the new technology. There's absolutely no credible evidence to support this. Still, investigating the conspiracy theory led me to the true story of what happened at Port Chicago and, eventually, to the writing of this book.

Step one for me was to read Dr. Robert Allen's remarkable book, *The Port Chicago Mutiny*. I then contacted Robert (he said I could call him that) and asked how I could find out more about this little-known chapter of civil rights history. After directing me to the scant supply of written sources, he suggested that if I really wanted to explore this story I should come to the memorial event held each year at the site of the Port Chicago disaster. A few Port Chicago veterans still attend, he explained, though at this point it's mostly younger generations of family members and friends.

I flew to San Francisco in July 2011, and not only did Robert drive me to the memorial event, he spent three days taking me around the Bay Area and introducing me to the amazing community of people who are working to keep the Port Chicago story alive. Spencer Sikes told me stories of his father, who served at Port Chicago, and shared his one-of-a-kind Port Chicago photo collection. Reverend Diana McDaniel told me about the work of the Friends of Port Chicago National Memorial—check this organization out online for lots more on the ongoing effort to exonerate the fifty sailors convicted of mutiny, and how to get involved.

At the end of my visit, Robert allowed me to make photocopies of the transcripts of the oral history interviews he conducted with Joseph Small and many of the other Port Chicago sailors. This is priceless material; it literally does not exist anywhere else. My deepest thanks to Robert for his generosity, encouragement, and helpful suggestions along the way.

Thanks to LT. S. B. Gaston, USN, for patiently answering many questions about naval ranks and terminology. Thanks also to the whole Roaring Brook and Macmillan team, especially Deirdre Langeland for her insightful and demanding (in a good way) edits, and Simon Boughton for his enthusiastic support for this project. Thanks to my longtime agent, Ken Wright, for helping to get this project going, and to Susan Cohen for so expertly taking over the reins. Thanks again to my friends at my unofficial office, the Saratoga Springs Public Library. And most of all, as always, thanks to my wife Rachel, for everything.

Picture Credits

3: Bettmann/Corbis/AP Images, 5: Getty Images, 6: Wikimedia Commons 8: Getty Images/Time-Life Pictures, 10: Naval Historical Center, Department of the Navy, official U.S. Navy photograph, photo 80-G-399009, 14: Courtesy Robert Allen, 17: U.S. Navy photograph, National Archives, 19: U.S. Navy photograph, National Archives, 22: U.S. Navy photograph, courtesy Port Chicago Naval Magazine National Memorial, POCH115, 30: U.S. Navy photograph, courtesy Port Chicago Naval Magazine National Memorial, POCH117, 32: U.S. Navy photograph, courtesy Port Chicago Naval Magazine National Memorial, POCH114, 33: U.S. Navy photograph, courtesy Port Chicago Naval Magazine National Memorial, POCH113, 35: U.S. Navy photograph, Courtesy Port Chicago Naval Magazine National Memorial, POCH117, 41: Library of Congress Prints & Photographs Division, NYWT&S Collection, LC-USZ62-112129, 49: Associated Press, 51: U.S. Navy photograph, courtesy Port Chicago Naval Magazine National Memorial, POCH110, 55: Courtesy Spencer Sikes II (son of Port Chicago explosion survivor), 56: Adapted from a diagram found in "Record of Proceedings of a Court of Inquiry Convened at the U.S. Naval Magazine, Port Chicago, California," July 21, 1944. Navy Judge Advocate General's Office, Washington, D.C., 60: U.S. Navy photograph, courtesy Port Chicago Naval Magazine National Memorial, POCH0064, 65: U.S. Navy photograph, courtesy Port Chicago Naval Magazine National Memorial, POCH92, 67: U.S. Navy photo. Courtesy Port Chicago Naval Magazine National Memorial. POCH 126, 68: Courtesy the *Shreveport Times,* 70: Associated Press, 72: AP Images, 74: A.P Photo/U.S. Navy, 79: Official U.S. Navy photograph, from the collection of the Naval Historical Center, 90: Oakland Tribune 10/17/1944. The Oakland Tribune Collection, the Oakland Museum of California. Gift of ANG Newspapers, 96: Copyright unknown, courtesy of Harry S. Truman Library, 98: Trial transcript, general court-martial, "Case of Julius J. Allen, Seaman Second Class, U.S. Naval Reserve at al.," September 14–October 24, 1944. Navy Judge Advocate General's Office, Washington, D.C., 106: Courtesy Robert Allen, 142: Trial transcript, general court-martial, "Case of Julius J. Allen, Seaman Second Class, U.S. Naval Reserve at al.," September 14–October 24, 1944. Navy Judge Advocate General's Office, Washington, D.C., 149: National Archives and Records Administration, 160: Prints and Photographs Division, Library of Congress, 162: Associated Press, 164: Courtesy Robert Allen, 166: Mike Kepka/*San Francisco Chronicle*/Corbis, 169: Associated Press

Index

Numbers in **bold** indicate pages with illustrations

A

African Americans: assignment after boot camp, expectation about, 20–21; assignments available to black servicemembers, 155–156; combat service and fighting, eagerness for, 20–21, 24, 50; dishonorable discharge for speaking out about racism, 75; eagerness to serve in Navy, 12–13, 21; fear of, 95–96, 124–125, 134–135, 136; Navy Cross award to, 4; Navy position available to, 1, 4, 6, 9, 11, 20–21; number of personnel at Port Chicago, 53; service of in wars before World War II, 6–9, **8**, 18; temperament and intelligence for handling explosives, 71, 95–96. *See also* segregation and racism
Allen, Robert, 165, 167
Ammunition, bombs, and explosives: accidental explosion, danger of, 33–34, 50, 52–54; betting on speed of loading duties, 48–49, 131, 135, 139, 145; black sailors assignment to loading duties, 21–25, 50, 95–96, 138–139, 145; dye capsule in bomb nose, 52; fear of black sailors about loading duties, 95–96, 124–125, 134–135, 136; feelings about handling, 25, 34; handling and loading duties, **22**, 23, 31–36, **32**, **33**, **35**, 47–49, **48–49**, 50–54, **51**, 55–57, **56**; hot cargo (incendiary bombs), 34, 57, 72; Marshall and questions about Port Chicago conditions, 144–145; pace and safety of loading duties,

47–49, 50–54, 69, 71, 77, 135, 139; punishment for men who returned to loading duties, 97, 101; refusal of loading duties at Mare Island, 76–86, 89, 90–92, 105–111, 115–122, 127–129, 168, 170; return to loading duties at Mare Island, 91–92; rough and careless handling as cause of explosion, 71; safety regulations for handling, 24; shift schedule for loading, 37, 50; training to handle, 20, 24–25, 139, 145; white sailors and ammunition loading duties, 96, 148; winch operations, 34–36, **35**. *See also* explosion at Port Chicago
Anthony, Douglas, 84–85
Armstrong, Daniel, 18
Army and Army Air Corps, **9**, 39–40

B

Bannon, Louis, 99–101
Barge prison: discussion between Small and Delucchi before boarding, 85–86, 125–126, 130; discussions between sailors aboard, 87–89, 99, 100, 101, 120–121, 126–127, 129–130, 139–140, 141; sailors transfer to, 85–90, 93, 133–134
Barracks: damage from explosion to, 58–59, **60–61**, 64; discussions about loading duties in, 100–101, 116–117, 121; injuries to sailors in, 58–59, 62–63, 64, 68; lights out activities, 57; list circulated in, 76, 117–118, 121, 125, 136
Bell, Rieves, 42–43
Blood supplies, 18
Bordenave, Martin: assignment after boot camp, expectation about, 20;

Bordenave, Martin (*continued*)
court-martial and sentence, 102;
defense strategy, 131; eagerness to
serve in Navy, 12; feelings about
importance of decision, 170;
prejudices against black sailors, 50;
refusal of loading duties, 91, 168
Bryan (E.A. Bryan), 53, 55–57, **56**, 66

C

Camp Shoemaker, 71–73, 93–94, 97,
141
Carr, Albert, 53–54
Civilian Conservation Corps, 13, 15
Civil rights: foundation of movement,
159, 161; Marshall role in fight for,
75, 160–161; Port Chicago 50 and
fight for, 168, 170
Coakley, James, 97, 99–101, 105–113,
115–123, 124, 127–130, 139–140,
150–151, 152
Combat service and fighting, eagerness
for, 20–21, 24, 50
Court-martial: appeal of verdict, 147,
150–152; closing arguments, 139–
141; cross-examination testimony,
107–110, 112–113, 117, 118, 119–
122, 127–130, 135, 136–138; defense
lawyers, 102–103, 105; defense
strategy and testimony, 123–132,
133–138; location of and setting
for, 104–105, **106–107**; Marshall
interest and involvement in, 114, 122,
130–131, 138–139; members of the
court, 104; overturning conviction,
165, 167–168; press coverage of, 105,
114–115, 135; prosecution lawyers,
97, 101, 105; prosecution strategy
and questioning, 105–113, 115–123,
150–151; reconsideration of case,
153–155, 167–168; rigging of against
accused men, 144; Small testimony,
123–130; testimony about Small,
118–121; transcript of, 144; verdict

and sentencing, 141–144, **142**, 146.
See also Port Chicago 50
Crittenden, Jack: eagerness to serve in
Navy, 12; pardon, feelings about, 168;
prison barge, 87; questioning
of about mutiny, 99; recovery of
bodies from explosion, 67; refusal of
loading duties as mutiny, 91; refusal
of loading duties at Mare Island, 85,
92; verdict and sentencing, 143

D

Delucchi, Ernest: accidental explosion,
danger of, 33–34; betting on speed of
loading duties, 48–49; character of,
29–30; conversation with Small about
prison barge, 85–86, 125–126, 130;
court-martial testimony, 110–113,
150, 151; opinions about, 29–30;
pace of loading duties, 53; refusal of
loading duties at Mare Island, 78–83,
91–92; Small promotion, opinion
about, 36
Dixson, Julius, 133–134, 141
Dunn, John, 133, 141

E

Edwards, Robert, 20, 38, 165, **166**
Explosion at Port Chicago: bravery
of black soldiers after blast, 69;
cause of, 69, 71, 72; compensation
for victims and families, 73–75;
deaths from, 66–67, 68; debris
from, 59–60, 61, 62; descriptions
of and damage from, 58–63, **60–61**;
injuries to sailors in barracks,
58–59, 62–63, 64, 68; inquiry into,
69, 71; investigation into, call by
Marshall for, 138–139; memorial
service for victims, **74**; pier and
ships, destruction of, 63, 64–69, **65**,
66–67, 70; real story about, interest
of sailors in, 155; recovery of bodies
from, 66–67

F

Flowers, Jefferson, 81, 134

Forrestal, James: appeal of verdict, 151–152; court-martial, interest in by, 114–115; integration of crews, 115, 146, 148–150, 153; Marshall and questions about Port Chicago conditions, 144–145; Marshall involvement in court-martial, 122; memo about explosion and recommendations for punishment, **98**; Navy policy toward black sailors, 114–115, 148–149; reconsideration of case, 153–155; white sailors and ammunition loading duties, 96, 148; Wright report to about black sailors, 95–96

Freedom, fighting for, 38

G

Gay, Willie, 50, 58, 81, 92

Goss, Nelson, 23, 68–69, 95

Granger, Lester, 149, **149**, 153

Gray, Joseph, 117–118

Great Lakes training center, 16–20, **17, 19**

Green, Edward, 45–46

Green, Nora, 45

Green, Oliver "Ollie," 134–135, 141

H

Harlem Hellfighters, **8**, 9

Henry, Frank, 136–137

"Honorable conditions" discharge, 163

I

Integration of military services, 115, 146, 148–150, 153, 155–156, 159–160

J

James, Joseph, 114

Jameson, DeWitt, 16, 66–67

Johnson, Edward, 116–117

K

King, Martin Luther, Jr., 161

Kinne, Merrill T., 47, 57, 62, 69, 71

Knox, Frank, 9–11, **10**, 20

L

Liberty days, 37–38, 42–43, 54–55, 157–158

M

Mare Island Naval Shipyard, refusal of loading duties at, 76–86, 89, 90–92, 91–92, 105–111, 115–122, 127–129, 168, 170

Marine Corps: African Americans in, 9; guard duty by marines, 53, 57, 83, 87, 88, 90, 91, 97, 99, 147; racial tensions between servicemembers, 148

Marshall, Thurgood, **41**; appeal of verdict, 147, 150–152; civil rights role, 75, 160–161; Constitution, memorization of, 44; early life of, 43–44; end of segregation in military services, reaction to, 156; interest and involvement in court-martial, 114, 122, 130–131, 138–139; investigation into explosion, call for, 138–139; NAACP attorney role, 42–43, 44–46, 75; Port Chicago conditions, questions about, 144–145; representation of black servicemen by, 42–43

McPherson, Alphonso, 85, 137

Meeks, Freddie, **72**, **162**; cause of explosion, 72; feelings about importance of decision, 170; handling and loading explosives, 33; life after leaving the Navy, 163; Marshall involvement in court-martial, 131; Port Chicago, appearance of area, 21, 23; presidential pardon for, 168; refusal of loading duties at Mare Island, 168; training to handle explosives, 24

Military services: integration of, 115, 146, 148–150, 153, 155–156, 159–160;

Military services (*continued*)
  morale of black servicemembers, 46;
  segregation and racism in, 7, 9–12,
  16–20, 23, 39–40, 46, 47; service of
  African Americans in wars before
  World War II, 6–9, 8, 18; tensions and
  friendships between servicemembers,
  147–148, 156–158
Miller, Dorie, 1–4, 3, 12, 18
Morehouse, Carleton, 83–84
Mutiny: charges of, 97; consequences
  of, 91; definition of, 92, 94–95, 140;
  evidence gathering and interrogations
  about, 97, 99–101, 137; refusal of
  loading duties as, 90–92, 94–95;
  Small's role in, 15, 93–95, 97, 99–101.
  See also court-martial; Port Chicago 50

N
National Association for the
  Advancement of Colored People
  (NAACP): founding of, 42; legal help
  for accused mutineers, 122, 130–131,
  138–139; Marshall as attorney for,
  42–43, 44–46, 75; pamphlet about
  prisoners, 146–147, 153; purpose of,
  42
Navy: assignments after boot camp, 12,
  20–21; danger of jobs in, 50; eagerness
  of African Americans to serve in, 12–
  13, 21; integration of crews, 115, 146,
  148–150, 153, 155–156, 159–160;
  number of African Americans in, 9;
  policy toward black sailors, 11–12,
  18, 95–96, 114–115, 131, 138–139,
  144–150; positions available to black,
  1, 4, 6, 9, 11, 20–21; refusal to obey
  orders, consequences of, 81–83, 84,
  92; segregation and racism in, 7,
  9–12, 16–20, 23, 39–40; tensions and
  friendships between black and white
  sailors, 147–148, 156–158
Navy Cross award, 2–4, 3
Nimitz, Chester, 3, 4

O
Osterhaus, Hugh, 104, 109–110, 124,
  135, 144, 151–152

P
Parks, Rosa, 161
Port Chicago 50: appeal of verdict,
  147, 150–152; daily activities for,
  147, 150; feelings about importance
  of decision, 168, 170; life after
  leaving the Navy, 161, 163–165;
  NAACP pamphlet about, 146–147,
  153; overturning conviction of, 165,
  167–168; presidential pardons for,
  167, 168; publicity about, 147, 153,
  167; release from prison and return
  to active duty, 153–155; respect for
  and treatment of, 147; sentencing
  after court-martial, 141–144, **142**,
  146. *See also* barge prison; court-
  martial; mutiny
Port Chicago Naval Magazine: African
  Americans assignment to, 12,
  21–25; appearance of area, 21, 23;
  commanding officer's feeling about
  minority personnel, 23–24; feelings
  about being assigned to, 23–25;
  importance of work at, 23–24, 49–50;
  morning routine at, 26, 29–30, **30–31**;
  number of personnel at, 53; transfer
  of black sailors from, 71–73. *See also*
  ammunition, bombs, and explosives
Prisoner sailors. *See* Port Chicago
  50

Q
Quinalt Victory, 55–57, **56**, 66, **66–67**

R
Rich, Morris, 60–61
Ringquist, Glen, 57, 59
Robinson, Jackie, 159, **160**
Robinson, Percy, **169**; assignment
  after boot camp, expectation about,

20–21; cause of explosion, 72; dye capsule in bomb nose, 52; eagerness to serve in Navy, 12; feelings about importance of decision, 168, 170; feelings about Navy experience, 165; frayed nerves of sailors, 73; Great Lakes training center experience, 16, 18; handling and loading explosives, 32, **48–49**; injury to from explosion, 58, 59, 62–63; journal kept by, **169**; life after leaving the Navy, 161, 163; mutiny and refusal to obey orders, 90–91; opinion about Delucchi, 29; pace of loading duties, 47; Port Chicago, appearance of area, 21; refusal of loading duties at Mare Island, 82, 83, 89, 168, 170; return to loading duties at Mare Island, 92

Roosevelt, Eleanor, 97, 153

Roosevelt, Franklin D., 6, 11, 97, 115

Roosevelt, Teddy, 7

Routh, Robert: feelings about being assigned to Port Chicago, 24; feelings about Navy experience, 165; foreboding about day, 53; Great Lakes training center experience, 16; injury to from explosion, 58, 59, 64; liberty days, 37; life after leaving the Navy, 161, 163; lights out activities, 57; Port Chicago, appearance of area, 21; recruitment of, 12–13; refusal of loading duties, feeling about, 94

S

Sangay, 78, 83–84, 105

Section Eight discharge, 26

Segregation and racism: desegregation on base, 89; discrimination against black sailors, 50, 73–75, 95–96; dishonorable discharge for speaking out about, 75; government inaction about, 46; Marshall and cases about, 42–43, 44–46, 75; Navy policy toward black sailors, 11–12, 18, 95–96, 114–115, 131, 138–139, 144–150; prejudices and segregation in the military, 7, 9–12, 16–20, 23, 39–40, 46, 47, 50, 95–96; in schools, 161; tensions and friendships between servicemembers, 147–148, 156–158; in towns near military bases, 37–38, 40, 45–46; treatment on liberty days, 37–38, 42–43, 157–158; unconstitutionality of segregation, 44. *See also* integration of military services

Sheppard, Cyril: assignment after boot camp, expectation about, 20; explosion and damage description, 59, 63; opinion about Delucchi, 29; pace of loading duties, 50; refusal of loading duties at Mare Island, 77; verdict and sentencing, 143

Sikes, Spencer, **55**; damage to barracks from explosion, 64; eagerness to serve in Navy, 21; feelings about handling explosives, 25; importance of work at Port Chicago, 49; liberty day, 54–55; mourning deaths from explosion, 71–72; reenlistment and Korean War service of, 160; return to Port Chicago after blast, 61–62

Small, Joseph "Joe," **14, 164**; accidental explosion, danger of, 33–34; assignment after boot camp, expectation about, 20; Camp Shoemaker brig, 93–94; CCC experience of, 13, 15; conversation with Delucchi about prison barge, 85–86, 125–126, 130; court-martial witness testimony about, 118–121; daily activities for prisoners, 147; death of, 168; defense strategy, 131–132; early life of, 27–29; explosion and damage description, 58–59; feelings about handling explosives, 34; feelings about importance of decision,

Small, Joseph (*continued*)
170; feelings about Navy experience,
165; frayed nerves of sailors, 73; Great
Lakes training center experience, 16;
handling and loading explosives, 32;
injuries to sailors from explosion, 62;
leadership abilities and role of, 15, 30,
36–37, 93, 97, 100–101, 123–130, 141;
liberty days, 37–38, 157–158; life after
leaving the Navy, 163–165; lights out
activities, 57; morning routine for, 26,
29; mutiny, understanding of, 94–95;
mutiny role of, 15, 93–95, 97, 99–101;
opinion about Delucchi, 29; pace of
loading duties, 48–49; pardons and
overturning conviction, feelings about,
167; path to Navy of, 13; petty officer
promotion, 36; prison barge, 87–89;
refusal of loading duties at Mare Island,
76, 77, 80–81, 82, 89, 92, 93–94, 170;
release from prison and return to active
duty, 154–155; respect for and opinions
about, 15, 29, 36; return to barracks
after shift, 54; tensions and friendships
between black and white sailors,
156–158; training to handle explosives,
24; transfer to Camp Shoemaker, 71;
transfer to Mare Island, 76; verdict and
sentencing, 143–144; winch operations,
34–36, 35; Wright meeting with, 93
Soublet, Morris, 24–25
Stubblefield, Edward, 118–121

T
Terminal Island Naval Disciplinary
Barracks, 144, 146–147

Tobin, James, 84–85, 99, 105–110,
133
Tobin, Joseph, 82–83
Trimmingham, Rupert, 40, 42
Truman, Harry, 156, 160
Tuskegee Air Field and training base,
39–40, 45

V
Veltmann, Gerald, **106–107**; closing
arguments, 140–141; court-martial
defense assignment, 102–103; cross-
examination testimony, 107–110,
112–113, 117, 118, 119–122; defense
strategy and testimony, 123–132, 133–
138; rigging of court-martial, 144

W
Waldrop, Edward, 97, 131, 144
Washington, George, 6–7, 6
West Virginia, 1–2
Williams, Albert, Jr., 12, 47, 59, 132,
163
World War I, 7–9, 8
World War II: declaration of war against
US, 5; end of, 152; Pearl Harbor
attack, 1–2, 5, 12; surrender of Japan,
152; US entrance into, 2, 4, 5–6
Wright, Carleton, **90**; appeal of verdict,
151–152; explosion, comments to
press about, 69; fear by black sailors,
95–96; mutiny and refusal to obey
orders, 90–91, 92; Navy policy toward
black sailors, 95–96; sentencing
following court-martial, 144; Small
meeting with, 93